THE MORAL ANIMAL

THE MORAL ANIMAL

Evolutionary Psychology
and Everyday Life

ROBERT WRIGHT

LITTLE, BROWN AND COMPANY

A *Little, Brown* Book

First published in the United States by Pantheon Books, 1994
This edition published by Little, Brown, 1995

A CIP catalogue record for this book
is available from the British Library.

ISBN 0 316 87501 5

Printed in England by Clays Ltd, St Ives plc

Little, Brown and Company (UK)
Brettenham House
Lancaster Place
London WC2E 7EN

For Lisa

Without thinking what he was doing, he took another drink of brandy. As the liquid touched his tongue he remembered his child, coming in out of the glare: the sullen unhappy knowledgeable face. He said, "Oh God, help her. Damn me, I deserve it, but let her soul live for ever." This was the love he should have felt for every soul in the world: all the fear and the wish to save concentrated unjustly on the one child. He began to weep; it was as if he had to watch her from the shore drown slowly because he had forgotten how to swim. He thought: This is what I should feel all the time for everyone . . .

– Graham Greene, *The Power and the Glory*

Contents

CONTENTS

THE MORAL ANIMAL

Introduction: **DARWIN AND US**

The Origin of Species contains almost no mention of the human species. The threats the book posed—to the biblical account of our creation, to the comforting belief that we are more than mere animals—were clear enough; Charles Darwin had nothing to gain by amplifying them. Near the end of the final chapter he simply suggested that, through the study of evolution, "light will be thrown on the origin of man and his history." And, in the same paragraph, he ventured that "in the distant future" the study of psychology "will be based on a new foundation."[1]

Distant was right. In 1960, 101 years after the *Origin* appeared, the historian John C. Greene observed, "With respect to the origin of man's distinctively human attributes, Darwin would be disappointed to find matters little advanced beyond his own speculations in *The Descent of Man*. He would be discouraged to hear J. S. Weiner of the Anthropology Laboratory at Oxford University describe this

3

subject as 'one large baffling topic on which our evolutionary insight remains meagre.' . . . In the current emphasis on man's uniqueness as a culture-transmitting animal Darwin might sense a tendency to return to the pre-evolutionary idea of an absolute distinction between man and other animals."[2]

A few years after Greene spoke, a revolution started. Between 1963 and 1974, four biologists—William Hamilton, George Williams, Robert Trivers, and John Maynard Smith—laid down a series of ideas that, taken together, refine and extend the theory of natural selection. These ideas have radically deepened the insight of evolutionary biologists into the social behavior of animals, including us.

At first, the relevance of the new ideas to our species was hazy. Biologists spoke confidently about the mathematics of self-sacrifice among ants, about the hidden logic of courtship among birds; but about human behavior they spoke conjecturally, if at all. Even the two epoch-marking books that synthesized and publicized the new ideas—E. O. Wilson's *Sociobiology* (1975) and Richard Dawkins's *The Selfish Gene* (1976)—said relatively little about humans. Dawkins steered almost entirely clear of the subject, and Wilson confined his discussion of our species to a final, slender, admittedly speculative chapter—28 pages out of 575.

Since the mid-1970s, the human angle has gotten much clearer. A small but growing group of scholars has taken what Wilson called "the new synthesis" and carried it into the social sciences with the aim of overhauling them. These scholars have applied the new, improved Darwinian theory to the human species, and then tested their applications with freshly gathered data. And along with their inevitable failures, they have had great success. Though they still consider themselves an embattled minority (an identity they seem sometimes to secretly enjoy), signs of their rising stature are clear. Venerable journals in anthropology, psychology, and psychiatry are publishing articles by authors who ten years ago were consigned to upstart journals of an expressly Darwinian bent. Slowly but unmistakably, a new worldview is emerging.

Here "worldview" is meant quite literally. The new Darwinian synthesis is, like quantum physics or molecular biology, a body of scientific theory and fact; but, unlike them, it is also a way of seeing everyday life. Once truly grasped (and it is much easier to grasp than either of them) it can entirely alter one's perception of social reality.

The questions addressed by the new view range from the mundane to the spiritual and touch on just about everything that matters: romance, love, sex (Are men and/or women really built for monogamy? What circumstances can make them more so or less so?); friendship and enmity (What is the evolutionary logic behind office politics—or, for that matter, politics in general?); selfishness, self-sacrifice, guilt (Why did natural selection give us that vast guilt repository known as the conscience? Is it truly a guide to "moral" behavior?); social status and social climbing (Is hierarchy inherent in human society?); the differing inclinations of men and women in areas such as friendship and ambition (Are we prisoners of our gender?); racism, xenophobia, war (Why do we so easily exclude large groups of people from the reach of our sympathy?); deception, self-deception, and the unconscious mind (Is intellectual honesty possible?); various psychopathologies (Is getting depressed, neurotic, or paranoid "natural"—and, if so, does that make it any more acceptable?); the love-hate relationship between siblings (Why isn't it pure love?); the tremendous capacity of parents to inflict psychic damage on their children (Whose interests do they have at heart?); and so on.

A QUIET REVOLUTION

The new Darwinian social scientists are fighting a doctrine that has dominated their fields for much of this century: the idea that biology doesn't much matter—that the uniquely malleable human mind, together with the unique force of culture, has severed our behavior from its evolutionary roots; that there is no inherent human nature driving human events, but that, rather, our essential nature is to be driven. As Emile Durkheim, the father of modern sociology, wrote at the turn of the century: human nature is "merely the indeterminate material that the social factor molds and transforms." History shows, said Durkheim, that even such deeply felt emotions as sexual jealousy, a father's love of his child, or the child's love of the father, are "far from being inherent in human nature." The mind, in this view, is basically passive—it is a basin into which, as a person matures, the local culture is gradually poured; if the mind sets any limits at all on the content of culture, they are exceedingly broad. The anthropologist Robert Lowie wrote in 1917 that "the principles of psychology are as incapable of accounting for the phenomena of culture as is gravitation to account for architectural styles."[3] Even psychologists—who might be expected to argue on behalf of the human mind—have often depicted it as little more than a blank slate. Behaviorism, which dominated psychology for a good part of this century, consists largely of the idea that people tend habitually to do what they are rewarded for doing and not do what they are punished for doing; thus is the formless mind given form. In B. F. Skinner's 1948 utopian novel *Walden II*, envy, jealousy, and other antisocial impulses were being eliminated via a strict regime of positive and negative reinforcements.

This view of human nature—as something that barely exists and doesn't much matter—is known among modern Darwinian social scientists as "the standard social science model."[4] Many of them learned it as undergraduates, and some of them spent years under its sway before beginning to question it. After a certain amount of questioning, they began to rebel.

In many ways, what is now happening fits Thomas Kuhn's description of a "paradigm shift" in his well-known book *The Structure of Scientific Revolutions*. A group of mainly young scholars have challenged the settled worldview of their elders, met with bitter resistance, persevered, and begun to flourish. Yet however classic this generational conflict may seem, it features a couple of distinctive ironies.

To begin with, it is, as revolutions go, inconspicuous. The various revolutionaries stubbornly refuse to call themselves by a single, simple name, the sort of thing that would fit easily onto a fluttering banner. They once had such a name—"sociobiology," Wilson's apt and useful term. But Wilson's book drew so much fire, provoked so many charges of malign political intent, so much caricature of sociobiology's substance, that the word became tainted. Most practitioners of the field he defined now prefer to avoid his label.[5] Though bound by allegiance to a compact and coherent set of doctrines, they go by different names: behavioral ecologists, Darwinian anthropologists, evolutionary psychologists, evolutionary psychiatrists. People sometimes ask: What ever happened to sociobiology? The answer is that it went underground, where it has been eating away at the foundations of academic orthodoxy.

The second irony of this revolution is tied to the first. Many features of the new view that the old guard most dislikes and fears are not, in fact, features of the new view. From the beginning, attacks on sociobiology were reflexive—reactions less to Wilson's book than to past books of a Darwinian cast. Evolutionary theory, after all, has a long and largely sordid history of application to human affairs. After being mingled with political philosophy around the turn of the century to form the vague ideology known as "social Darwinism," it played into the hands of racists, fascists, and the most heartless sort of capitalists. It also, around that time, spawned some simplistic ideas about the hereditary basis of behavior—ideas that, conveniently, fed these very political misuses of Darwinism. The resulting aura—of crudeness, both intellectual and ideological—continues to cling to Darwinism in the minds of many academics and laypersons. (Some people think the term Darwinism *means* social Darwinism.) Hence many misconceptions about the new Darwinian paradigm.

INVISIBLE UNITIES

For example: the new Darwinism is often mistaken for an exercise in social division. Around the turn of the century, anthropologists spoke casually of the "lower races," of "savages" who were beyond moral improvement. To the uncritical observer, such attitudes seemed to fit easily enough into a Darwinian framework, as would later supremacist doctrines, including Hitler's. But today's Darwinian anthropologists, in scanning the world's peoples, focus less on surface differences among cultures than on deep unities. Beneath the global crazy quilt of rituals and customs, they see recurring patterns in the structure of family, friendship, politics, courtship, morality. They believe the evolutionary design of human beings explains these patterns: why people in all cultures worry about social status (often more than they realize); why people in all cultures not only gossip, but gossip about the same kinds of things; why in all cultures men and women seem different in a few basic ways; why people everywhere feel guilt, and feel it in broadly predictable circumstances; why people everywhere have a deep sense of justice, so that the axioms "One good turn deserves another" and "An eye for an eye, a tooth for a tooth" shape human life everywhere on this planet.

In a way, it's not surprising that the rediscovery of human nature has taken so long. Being everywhere we look, it tends to elude us. We take for granted such bedrock elements of life as gratitude, shame, remorse, pride, honor, retribution, empathy, love, and so on—just as we take for granted the air we breathe, the tendency of d.opped objects to fall, and other standard features of living on this planet.[6] But things didn't have to be this way. We could live on a planet where social life featured none of the above. We could live on a planet where some ethnic groups felt some of the above and others felt others. But we don't. The more closely Darwinian anthropologists look at the world's peoples, the more they are struck by the dense and intricate web of human nature by which all are bound. And the more they see how the web was woven.

Even when the new Darwinians *do* focus on differences—whether among groups of people or among people within groups—they are not generally inclined to explain them in terms of genetic differences. Darwinian anthropologists see the world's undeniably diverse cultures as products of a single human nature responding to widely varying circumstances; evolutionary theory reveals previously invisible links between the circumstances and the cultures (explaining, for example, why some cultures have dowry and others don't). And evolutionary psychologists, contrary to common expectation, subscribe to a cardinal doctrine of twentieth-century psychology and psychiatry: the potency of early social environment in shaping the adult mind. Indeed, a few are preoccupied with this subject, determined to uncover basic laws of psychological development and convinced that they can do so only with Darwinian tools. If we want to know, say, how levels of ambition or of insecurity get adjusted by early experience, we must first ask why natural selection made them adjustable.

This isn't to say that human behavior is infinitely malleable. In tracing the channels of environmental influence, most evolutionary psychologists see some firm banks. The utopian spirit of B. F. Skinner's behaviorism, the sense that a human being can become any sort of animal at all with proper conditioning, is not faring well these days. Still, neither is the idea that the grimmest parts of the human experience are wholly immutable, grounded in "instincts" and "innate drives"; nor the idea that psychological differences among people boil down mainly to genetic differences. They boil down to the *genes*, of course (where else could rules for mental development ultimately reside?), but not necessarily to *differences* in genes. A guiding assumption of many evolutionary psychologists, for reasons we'll come to, is that the most radical differences among people are the ones most likely to be traceable to environment.

In a sense, evolutionary psychologists are trying to discern a second level of human nature, a deeper unity within the species. First the anthropologist notes recurring themes in culture after culture: a thirst for social approval, a capacity for guilt. You might call these, and many other such universals, "the knobs of human nature." Then the psychologist notes that the exact tunings of the knobs seem to differ from person to person. One person's "thirst for approval" knob is set in the comfort zone, down around (relatively) "self-assured," and another person's is up in the excruciating "massively insecure" zone; one person's guilt knob is set low and another person's is painfully high. So the psychologist asks: How do these knobs get set? Genetic differences among individuals surely play a role, but perhaps a larger role is played by genetic commonalities: by a generic, species-wide developmental program that absorbs information from the social environment and adjusts the maturing mind accordingly. Oddly, future progress in grasping the importance of environment will probably come from thinking about genes.

Thus, human nature comes in two forms, both of which have a natural tendency to get ignored. First, there's the kind that's so pervasively apparent as to be taken for granted (guilt, for example). Second, there's the kind whose very function is to generate differences among people as they grow up, and thus naturally conceals itself (a developmental program that *calibrates* guilt). Human nature consists of knobs and of mechanisms for tuning the knobs, and both are invisible in their own way.

There is another source of invisibility, another reason human nature has been slow to come to light: the basic evolutionary logic common to people everywhere is opaque to introspection. Natural selection appears to have hidden our true selves from our conscious selves. As Freud saw, we are oblivious to our deepest motivations—but in ways more chronic and complete (and even, in some cases, more grotesque) than he imagined.

DARWINIAN SELF-HELP

Though this book will touch on many behavioral sciences—anthropology, psychiatry, sociology, political science—evolutionary psychology will be at its center. This young and still inchoate discipline, with its partly fulfilled promise of creating a whole new science of mind, lets us now ask a question that couldn't have been profitably asked in 1859, after the *Origin* appeared, nor in 1959: What does the theory of natural selection have to offer ordinary human beings?

For example: Can a Darwinian understanding of human nature help people reach their goals in life? Indeed, can it help them choose their goals? Can it help distinguish between practical and impractical goals? More profoundly, can it help in deciding which goals are worthy? That is, does knowing how evolution has shaped our basic moral impulses help us decide which impulses we should consider legitimate?

The answers, in my opinion, are: yes, yes, yes, yes, and, finally, yes. The preceding sentence will annoy, if not outrage, many people in the field. (Believe me. I've shown it to some of them.) They have long had to labor under the burden of Darwinism's past moral and political misuses, and they would like to keep the realms of science and value separate. You can't derive basic moral values from natural selection, they say, or indeed from any of nature's workings. If you do, you're committing what philosophers call "the naturalistic fallacy"—the unwarranted inference of "ought" from "is."

I agree: nature isn't a moral authority, and we needn't adopt any "values" that seem implicit in its workings—such as "might makes right." Still, a true understanding of human nature will inevitably affect moral thought deeply and, as I will try to show, legitimately.

This book, with its relevance to questions of everyday life, will have some features of a self-help book. But it will lack many. The next several hundred pages aren't loaded with pithy advice and warm reassurance. A Darwinian viewpoint won't hugely simplify your life, and in some ways will complicate it, by shining harsh light on morally dubious behaviors to which we are prone and whose dubiousness evolution has conveniently hidden from us. The few crisp and upbeat prescriptions I can glean from the new Darwinian paradigm are more than matched by the stubborn and weighty trade-offs, dilemmas, and conundrums it illuminates.

But you can't deny the intensity of the illumination—at least you won't, I hope, be denying it by the end of the book. Although one of my aims is to find practical applications of evolutionary psychology, the prior and central aim is to cover the basic principles of evolutionary psychology—to show how elegantly the theory of natural selection, as understood today, reveals the contours of the human mind. This book is, first, a sales pitch for a new science; only secondarily is it a sales pitch for a new basis of political and moral philosophy.

I've taken pains to keep these two issues separate, to distinguish between the new Darwinism's claims about the human mind and my own claims about the practical emanations of the new Darwinism. Many people who buy the first set of claims, the scientific set, will no doubt reject much of the second set, the philosophical set. But I think few people who buy the first set will deny its relevance to the second set. It is hard, on the one hand, to agree that the new paradigm is by far the most powerful lens through which to look at the human species and then to set the lens aside when examining the human predicament. The human species *is* the human predicament.

DARWIN, SMILES, AND MILL

The Origin of Species wasn't the only seminal book published in England in 1859. There was also the best-selling and genre-christening *Self-Help*, written by the journalist Samuel Smiles. And then there was *On Liberty*, by John Stuart Mill. As it happens, these two books nicely frame the question of what Darwin's book will ultimately come to mean.

Self-Help didn't stress getting in touch with your feelings, extricating yourself from sour relationships, tapping into harmonic cosmic forces, or the various other things that have since given self-help books an air of self-absorption and facile comfort. It preached essential Victorian virtues: civility, integrity, industry, perseverance, and, undergirding them all, iron self-control. A man, Smiles believed, can achieve almost anything "by the exercise of his own free powers of action and self-denial." But he must be ever "armed against the temptation of low indulgences," and must not "defile his body by sensuality, nor his mind by servile thoughts."[7]

On Liberty, by contrast, was a strong polemic against the stifling Victorian insistence on self-restraint and moral conformity. Mill indicted Christianity, with its "horror of sensuality," and complained that " 'thou shalt not' predominates unduly over 'thou shalt.' " He found especially deadening the Calvinist branch, with its belief that, "human nature being radically corrupt, there is no redemption for any one until human nature is killed within him." Mill took a sunnier view of human nature, and suggested that Christianity do the same. "[I]f it be any part of religion to believe that man was made by a good Being, it is more consistent with that faith to believe, that this Being gave all human faculties that they might be cultivated and unfolded, not rooted out and consumed, and that he takes delight in every nearer approach made by his creatures to the ideal conception embodied in them, every increase in any of their capabilities of comprehension, of action, or of enjoyment."[8]

Characteristically, Mill had hit on an important question: Are people inherently bad? Those who believe so have tended, like Samuel Smiles, to be morally conservative—to stress self-denial, abstinence, taming the beast within. Those who believe not have tended, like Mill, to be morally liberal, fairly relaxed about how people choose to behave. Evolutionary psychology, young though it is, has already shed much light on this debate. Its findings are at once comforting and unsettling.

Altruism, compassion, empathy, love, conscience, the sense of justice—all of these things, the things that hold society together, the things that allow our species to think so highly of itself, can now confidently be said to have a firm genetic basis. That's the good news. The bad news is that, although these things are in some ways blessings for humanity as a whole, they didn't evolve for the "good of the species" and aren't reliably employed to that end. Quite the contrary: it is now clearer than ever how (and precisely *why*) the moral sentiments are used with brutal flexibility, switched on and off in keeping with self-interest; and how naturally oblivious we often are to this switching. In the new view, human beings are a species splendid in their array of moral equipment, tragic in their propensity to misuse it, and pathetic in their constitutional ignorance of the misuse. The title of this book is not wholly without irony.

Thus, for all the emphasis in popular treatments of sociobiology on the "biological basis of altruism," and for all its genuine importance, the idea that John Stuart Mill ridiculed—of a corrupt human nature, of "original sin"—doesn't deserve such summary dismissal. And for that reason, I believe, neither does moral conservatism. Indeed, I believe some—*some*—of the conservative norms that prevailed in Victorian England reflect, if obliquely, a surer grasp of human nature than has prevailed in the social sciences for most of this century; and that *some* of the resurgent moral conservatism of the past decade, especially in the realm of sex, rests on an implicit rediscovery of truths about human nature that have long been denied.

If modern Darwinism indeed has some morally conservative emanations, does that mean it has politically conservative emanations? This is a tricky and important question. It's easy enough, and correct, to dismiss social Darwinism as a spasm of malicious confusion. But the question of innate human goodness casts a political shadow that can't be so casually disregarded, for linkage between ideology and views on human nature has a long and distinguished history. Over the past two centuries, as the meanings of political "liberalism" and "conservatism" have changed almost beyond recognition, one distinction between the two has endured: political liberals (such as Mill, in his day) tend to take a rosier view of human nature than conservatives, and to favor a looser moral climate.

Still, it isn't clear that this connection between morals and politics is truly necessary, especially in a modern context. To the extent that the new Darwinian paradigm has reasonably distinct political implications—and as a general rule it just doesn't—they are about as often to the left as to the right. In some ways they are radically to the left.

(Though Karl Marx would find much to dislike in the new paradigm, he would find parts of it very appealing.) What's more, the new paradigm suggests reasons a modern political liberal might subscribe to some morally conservative doctrines as a matter of ideological consistency. At the same time, it suggests that a conservative moral agenda may at times profit from liberal social policies.

DARWINIZING DARWIN

In making the case for a Darwinian outlook, I will use, as Exhibit A, Charles Darwin. His thoughts, emotions, and behavior will illustrate the principles of evolutionary psychology. In 1876, in the first paragraph of his autobiography, Darwin wrote, "I have attempted to write the following account of myself, as if I were a dead man in another world looking back at my own life." (He added, with characteristic grim detachment, "Nor have I found this difficult, for life is nearly over with me.")[9] I like to think that if Darwin were looking back today, with the penetrating hindsight afforded by the new Darwinism, he would see his life somewhat as I'll be depicting it.

Darwin's life will serve as more than illustration. It will be a miniature test of the explanatory power of the modern, refined version of his theory of natural selection. Advocates of evolutionary theory—including him, including me—have long claimed that it is so powerful as to explain the nature of all living things. If we're right, the life of any human being, selected at random, should assume new clarity when looked at from this viewpoint. Well, Darwin hasn't exactly been selected at random, but he'll do as a guinea pig. My claim is that his life—and his social environment, Victorian England—make more sense when looked at from a Darwinian vantage point than from any competing perspective. In this respect, he and his milieu are like all other organic phenomena.

Darwin doesn't *seem* like other organic phenomena. The things that come to mind when we think of natural selection—the ruthless pursuit of genetic self-interest, survival of the fiercest—don't come to mind when we think of Darwin. By all accounts, he was enormously civil and humane (except, perhaps, when circumstance made it hard to be both; he could grow agitated while denouncing slavery,

and he might lose his temper if he saw a coachman abusing a horse).[10]
His gentleness of manner and his utter lack of pretense, well marked
from his youth, were uncorrupted by fame. "[O]f all eminent men
that I have ever seen he is beyond comparison the most attractive to
me," observed the literary critic Leslie Stephen. "There is something
almost pathetic in his simplicity and friendliness."[11] Darwin was, to
borrow a phrase from the title of *Self-Help*'s last chapter, a "true
gentleman."

Darwin read *Self-Help*. But he needn't have. By then (age fifty-
one) he was already a walking embodiment of Smiles's dictum that
life is a battle against "moral ignorance, selfishness, and vice." Indeed,
one common view is that Darwin was decent to a fault—that, if he
needed a self-help book, it was a self-help book of the late-twentieth-
century variety, something about how to feel good about yourself,
how to look out for number one. The late John Bowlby, one of
Darwin's most perceptive biographers, believed that Darwin suf-
fered from "nagging self-contempt" and an "overactive conscience."
Bowlby wrote: "While there is so much to admire in the absence of
pretension and in the strong moral principles that were an integral
part of Darwin's character and that, with much else, endeared him
to relatives, friends and colleagues, these qualities were unfortunately
developed prematurely and to excessive degree."[12]

Darwin's "excessive" humility and morality, his extreme lack of
brutishness, are what make him so valuable as a test case. I will try
to show that natural selection, however seemingly alien to his character, can account for it. It is true that Darwin was as gentle, humane,
and decent a man as you can reasonably hope to find on this planet.
But it is also true that he was fundamentally no different from the
rest of us. Even Charles Darwin was an animal.

Part One: **SEX, ROMANCE, AND LOVE**

Chapter 1: DARWIN COMES OF AGE

*As for an English lady, I have almost forgotten what she is.—
something very angelic and good.*
                              —Letter from the HMS *Beagle* (1835)[1]

Boys growing up in nineteenth-century England weren't generally advised to seek sexual excitement. And they weren't advised to do things that might lead them to think about seeking it. The Victorian physician William Acton, in his book *The Functions and Disorders of the Reproductive Organs,* warned about exposing a boy to the "classical works" of literature. "He reads in them of the pleasures, nothing of the penalties, of sexual indulgences. He is not intuitively aware that, if the sexual desires are excited, it will require greater power of will to master them than falls to the lot of most lads; that if indulged in, the man will and must pay the penalty for the errors of the boy; that for one that escapes, ten will suffer; that an awful risk attends abnormal substitutes for sexual intercourse; and that self-indulgence, long pursued, tends ultimately, if carried far enough, to early death or self-destruction."[2]

Acton's book was published in 1857, during the mid-Victorian period whose moral tenor it exudes. But sexual repression had long been in the air—before Victoria's ascent to the throne in 1837, even before the date more loosely used to bracket the Victorian era, 1830. Indeed, at the turn of the century, the Evangelical movement that so nourished the new moral austerity was well under way.[3] As G. M. Young noted in *Portrait of an Age*, a boy born in England in 1810—the year after Darwin's birth—"found himself at every turn controlled, and animated, by the imponderable pressure of the Evangelical discipline. . . . " This was not a matter only of sexual restraint, but of restraint generally—an all-out vigilance against indulgence. The boy would learn, as Young put it, that "the world is very evil. An unguarded look, a word, a gesture, a picture, or a novel, might plant a seed of corruption in the most innocent heart. . . . "[4] Another student of Victorianism has described "a life of constant struggle—both to resist temptation and to master the desires of the ego"; by "an elaborate practice of self-discipline, one had to lay the foundation of good habits and acquire the power of self-control."[5]

It was this view that Samuel Smiles, born three years after Darwin, would package in *Self-Help*. As the book's wide success attests, the Evangelical outlook spread well beyond the walls of the Methodist churches that were its wellspring, into the homes of Anglicans, Unitarians, and even agnostics.[6] The Darwin household is a good example. It was Unitarian (and Darwin's father was a freethinker, if a quiet one), yet Darwin absorbed the puritanical strain of his time. It is visible in his burdensome conscience and in the astringent code of conduct he championed. Long after he had given up his faith, he wrote that "the highest stage in moral culture at which we can arrive, is when we recognise that we ought to control our thoughts, and [as Tennyson said] 'not even in inmost thought to think again the sins that made the past so pleasant to us.' Whatever makes any bad action familiar to the mind, renders its performance by so much the easier. As Marcus Aurelius long ago said, 'Such as are thy habitual thoughts, such also will be the character of thy mind; for the soul is dyed by the thoughts.' "[7]

Though Darwin's youth and life were in some ways eccentric, in this one sense they were typical of his era: he lived amid tremendous moral gravity. His world was a place where questions of right and wrong were seen at every turn. What's more, it was a place where these questions seemed answerable—absolutely answerable—though the answers were sometimes painful to bear. It was a world very different from ours, and Darwin's work would do much to make the difference.

AN UNLIKELY HERO

The original career plan for Charles Darwin was to be a doctor. His father, he recalled, felt sure "that I should make a successful physician—meaning by this, one who got many patients." The senior Darwin, himself a successful physician, "maintained that the chief element of success was exciting confidence; but what he saw in me which convinced him that I should create confidence I know not." Nonetheless, Charles at age sixteen dutifully left the cozy family estate in Shrewsbury and, accompanied by his older brother, Erasmus, headed for the University of Edinburgh to study medicine.

Enthusiasm for this calling failed to materialize. At Edinburgh Darwin paid grudging attention to course work, avoided the operating theater (watching surgery, in the days before chloroform, wasn't his cup of tea), and spent much time on extracurricular pursuits: trawling with fishermen to gather oysters, which he then dissected; taking taxidermy lessons to complement his newfound love of hunting; walking and talking with a sponge expert named Robert Grant, who ardently believed in evolution—but didn't, of course, know how it works.

Darwin's father sensed a certain vocational drift and, Charles recalled, "was very properly vehement against my turning an idle sporting man, which then seemed my probable destination."[8] Hence Plan B. Dr. Darwin proposed a career in the clergy.

This may seem strange guidance, coming from a man who didn't believe in God, given to a son who wasn't glaringly devout and who had a more obvious calling in zoology. But Darwin's father was a practical man. And in those days zoology and theology were two sides of one coin. If all living things were God's handiwork, then the study of their ingenious design was the study of God's genius. The most noted proponent of this view was William Paley, author of the 1802 book *Natural Theology; or, evidences of the existence and attributes of the Deity, collected from the appearances of nature.* In it Paley argued that, just as a watch implies a watchmaker, a world full of intricately designed organisms, precisely suited to their tasks, implies a designer.[9] (He was right. The question is whether the designer is a farseeing God or an unconscious process.)

The workaday upshot of natural theology was that a country parson could, without guilt, spend much of his time studying and writing about nature. Hence, perhaps, Darwin's fairly favorable, if not especially spiritual, reaction to the prospect of donning the cloth. "I asked for some time to consider, as from what little I had heard and thought on the subject I had scruples about declaring my belief in all the dogmas of the Church of England; though otherwise I liked the thought of being a country clergyman." He did some reading on divinity and "as I did not then in the least doubt the strict and literal truth of every word in the Bible, I soon persuaded myself that our Creed must be fully accepted." To prepare for the clergy, Darwin went to Cambridge University, where he read his Paley and was "charmed and convinced by the long line of argumentation."[10]

Not for long. Just after finishing at Cambridge, Darwin encountered a strange opportunity: to serve as naturalist aboard the HMS *Beagle.* The rest, of course, is history. Though Darwin didn't conceive of natural selection aboard the *Beagle,* his study of wildlife around the world convinced him that evolution had taken place, and alerted him to some of its most suggestive properties. Two years after the end of the ship's five-year voyage, he saw how evolution works. Darwin's plans to enter the clergy would not survive this insight. As if to provide future biographers with ample symbolism, he had brought along on the voyage his favorite volume of verse, *Paradise Lost.*[11]

As Darwin left England's shores, there was no glaring reason to think people would be writing books about him a century and a half later. His youth, ventured one biographer, in a fairly common judgment, had been "unmarked by the slightest trace of genius."[12] Of course, such claims are always suspect, as the early inauspiciousness of great minds makes for good reading. And this particular claim deserves special doubt, as it rests largely on Darwin's self-appraisals, which didn't tend toward inflation. Darwin reports that he couldn't master foreign languages, and struggled with mathematics, and "was considered by all my masters and by my Father as a very ordinary boy, rather below the common standard in intellect." Maybe, maybe not. Perhaps more stock should be placed in another of his appraisals, about his knack for winning the friendship of men "so much older than me and higher in academical position": "I infer that there must have been something in me a little superior to the common run of youths."[13]

Anyway, the absence of blinding intellectual flash isn't the only thing that has led some biographers to deem Darwin "an unlikely survivor in the immortality stakes."[14] There is also the sense that he just wasn't a formidable man. He was so decent, so sweet, so lacking in untrammeled ambition. And he was something of a country boy, a bit insular and simple. One writer has asked, "Why was it given to Darwin, less ambitious, less imaginative, and less learned than many of his colleagues, to discover the theory sought after by others so assiduously? How did it come about that one so limited intellectually and insensitive culturally should have devised a theory so massive in structure and sweeping in significance?"[15]

One way to answer that question is by contesting its assessment of Darwin (an exercise we'll get to), but an easier way is to contest its assessment of his theory. The idea of natural selection, while indeed "sweeping in significance," is not really "massive in structure." It is a small and simple theory, and it didn't take a huge intellect to conceive it. Thomas Henry Huxley, Darwin's good friend, staunch defender, and fluent popularizer, supposedly chastised himself upon comprehending the theory, exclaiming, "How extremely stupid not to have thought of that!"[16]

All the theory of natural selection says is the following. If within a species there is variation among individuals in their hereditary traits, and some traits are more conducive to survival and reproduction than others, then those traits will (obviously) become more widespread within the population. The result (obviously) is that the species' aggregate pool of hereditary traits changes. And there you have it.

Of course, the change may seem negligible within any given generation. If long necks help animals reach precious leaves, and shorter-necked animals therefore die before reproducing, the species' average neck size barely grows. Still, if variation in neck size arises freshly with new generations (through sexual recombination or genetic mutation, we now know), so that natural selection continues to have a range of neck sizes to "choose" from, then average neck size will keep creeping upward. Eventually, a species that started out with horselike necks will have giraffe-like necks. It will, in other words, be a new species.

Darwin once summed up natural selection in ten words: "[M]ultiply, vary, let the strongest live and the weakest die."[17] Here "strongest," as he well knew, means not just brawniest, but best adapted to the environment, whether through camouflage, cleverness, or anything else that aids survival and reproduction.* The word *fittest* (a coinage Darwin didn't make but did accept) is typically used in place of *strongest,* signifying this broader conception—an organism's "fitness" to the task of transmitting its genes to the next generation, within its particular environment. "Fitness" is the thing that natural selection, in continually redesigning species, perpetually "seeks" to maximize. Fitness is what made us what we are today.

If this seems easy to believe, you probably aren't getting the picture. Your entire body—much more complexly harmonious than any product of human design—was created by hundreds of thousands of incremental advances, and *each increment was an accident;* each tiny step between your ancestral bacterium and you *just happened* to help some intermediate ancestor more profusely get its genes into the next generation. Creationists sometimes say that the odds of a person being produced through random genetic change are about equal to those of a monkey typing the works of Shakespeare. Well, yes. Not the complete works, maybe, but certainly some long, recognizable stretches.

Still, things this unlikely can, through the logic of natural selec-

---

*Actually, Darwin divided the "survival" and "reproductive" aspects of the process. Traits leading to successful mating he attributed to "sexual selection," as distinct from natural selection. But these days, natural selection is often defined broadly, to encompass both aspects: the preservation of traits that are in any way conducive to getting an organism's genes into the next generation.

tion, be rendered plausible. Suppose a single ape gets some lucky break—gene XL, say, which imbues parents with an ounce of extra love for their offspring, love that translates into slightly more assiduous nurturing. In the life of any one ape, that gene probably won't be crucial. But suppose that, *on average*, the offspring of apes with the XL gene are 1 percent more likely to survive to maturity than the offspring of apes without it. So long as this thin advantage holds, the fraction of apes with gene XL will tend to grow, and the fraction without it will tend to shrink, generation by generation by generation. The eventual culmination of this trend is a population in which all animals have the XL gene. The gene, at that point, will have reached "fixation"; a slightly higher degree of parental love will be "species typical" now than before.

Okay, so one lucky break thus flourishes. But how likely is it that the luck will persist—that the *next* random genetic change will *further* increase the amount of parental love? How likely is the "XL" mutation to be followed by an "XXL" mutation? Not at all likely in the case of any one ape. But within the population there are now scads of apes with the XL gene. If any one of them, or any one of their offspring, or grand-offspring, happens to luck out and get the XXL gene, the gene will have a good chance of spreading, if slowly, through the population. Of course, in the meantime, lots more apes will probably get various less auspicious genes, and some of those genes may extinguish the lineage in which they appear. Well, that's life.

Thus does natural selection beat the odds—by not really beating them. The thing that is massively more probable than the charmed lineages that populate the world today—an uncharmed lineage, which reaches a dead end through an unlucky break—happened a massively larger number of times. The dustbin of genetic history overflows with failed experiments, long strings of code that were as vibrant as Shakespearean verse *until* that fateful burst of gibberish. Their disposal is the price paid for design by trial and error. But so long as that price can be paid—so long as natural selection has enough generations to work on, and can cast aside scores of failed experiments for every one it preserves—its creations can be awesome. Natural selection is an inanimate process, devoid of consciousness, yet is a tireless refiner, an ingenious craftsman.*

Every organ inside you is testament to its art—your heart, your lungs, your stomach. All these are "adaptations"—fine products of inadvertent design, mechanisms that are here because they have in the past contributed to your ancestors' fitness. And all are species-typical. Though one person's lungs may differ from another's, sometimes for genetic reasons, almost all the genes involved in lung construction are the same in you as in your next-door neighbor, as in an Eskimo, as in a pygmy. The evolutionary psychologists John Tooby and Leda Cosmides have noted that every page of *Gray's Anatomy* applies to all peoples in the world. Why, they have gone on to ask, should the anatomy of the mind be any different? The working thesis of evolutionary psychology is that the various "mental organs" constituting the human mind—such as an organ inclining people to love their offspring—are species-typical.[18] Evolutionary psychologists are pursuing what is known in the trade as "the psychic unity of humankind."

CLIMATE CONTROL

Between us and the australopithecine, which walked upright but had an ape-sized brain, stand a few million years: 100,000, maybe 200,000 generations. That may not sound like much. But it has taken only around 5,000 generations to turn a wolf into a chihuahua—and, at the same time, along a separate line, into a Saint Bernard. Of course, dogs evolved by artificial, not natural, selection. But as Darwin stressed, the two are essentially the same; in both cases traits are weeded out of a population by criteria that persist for many generations. And in both cases, if the "selective pressure" is strong enough—if genes are weeded out fast enough—evolution can proceed briskly.

One might wonder how the selective pressure could have been

---

*In this book I will sometimes talk about what natural selection "wants" or "intends," or about what "values" are implicit in its workings. I'll always use quotation marks, since these are just metaphors. But the metaphors are worth using, I believe, because they help us come to moral terms with Darwinism.

very strong during recent human evolution. After all, what usually generates the pressure is a hostile environment—droughts, ice ages, tough predators, scarce prey—and as human evolution has proceeded, the relevance of these things has abated. The invention of tools, of fire, the advent of planning and cooperative hunting—these brought growing control over the environment, growing insulation from the whims of nature. How, then, did ape brains turn into human brains in a few million years?

Much of the answer seems to be that the environment of human evolution has been human (or prehuman) beings.[19] The various members of a Stone Age society were each other's rivals in the contest to fill the next generation with genes. What's more, they were each other's tools in that contest. Spreading their genes depended on dealing with their neighbors: sometimes helping them, sometimes ignoring them, sometimes exploiting them, sometimes liking them, sometimes hating them—and having a sense for which people warrant which sort of treatment, and when they warrant it. The evolution of human beings has consisted largely of adaptation to one another.

Since each adaptation, having fixed itself in the population, thus changes the social environment, adaptation only invites more adaptation. Once all parents have the XXL gene, it gives no parent an edge in the ongoing contest to create the most viable and prolific offspring. The arms race continues. In this case, it's an arms race of love. Often, it's not.

It is fashionable in some circles to downplay the whole idea of adaptation, of coherent evolutionary design. Popularizers of biological thought often emphasize not the role of fitness in evolutionary change but the role of randomness and happenstance. Some climate shift may come out of the blue and extinguish unlucky species of flora and fauna, changing the whole context of evolution for any species lucky enough to survive the calamity. A roll of the cosmic dice and suddenly all bets are off. Certainly that happens, and this is indeed one sense in which "randomness" greatly affects evolution. There are other senses as well. For example, new traits on which natural selection passes judgment seem to be randomly generated.[20]

But none of the "randomness" in natural selection should be allowed to obscure its central feature: that the overriding criterion of organic design is fitness. Yes, the dice do get rerolled, and the context of evolution changes. A feature that is adaptive today may not be adaptive tomorrow. So natural selection often finds itself amending outmoded features. This ongoing adjustment to circumstance can give organic life a certain jerry-built quality. (It's the reason people have back trouble; if you were designing a walking organism from scratch rather than incrementally adapting a former tree-dweller, you would never have built such bad backs.) Nonetheless, changes in circumstance are typically gradual enough for evolution to keep pace (even if it has to break into a trot now and then, when selective pressure becomes severe), and it often does so ingeniously.

And all along the way, its definition of good design remains the same. The thousands and thousands of genes that influence human behavior—genes that build the brain and govern neurotransmitters and other hormones, thus defining our "mental organs"—are here for a reason. And the reason is that they goaded our ancestors into getting their genes into the next generation. If the theory of natural selection is correct, then essentially everything about the human mind should be intelligible in these terms. The basic ways we feel about each other, the basic kinds of things we think about each other and say to each other, are with us today by virtue of their past contribution to genetic fitness.

DARWIN'S SEX LIFE

No human behavior affects the transmission of genes more obviously than sex. So no parts of human psychology are clearer candidates for evolutionary explanation than the states of mind that lead to sex: raw lust, dreamy infatuation, sturdy (or at least sturdy-feeling) love, and so on—the basic forces amid which people all over the world, including Charles Darwin, have come of age.

When Darwin left England he was twenty-two and, presumably, flooded with the hormones that young men are, by design, flooded with. He had been sweet on a couple of local girls, especially the pretty, popular, and highly coquettish Fanny Owen. He once let her shoot a hunting gun, and she looked so charming, gamely pretending its kick hadn't hurt her shoulder, that he would recall the incident decades later with evident fondness.[21] From Cambridge he conducted a tenuous flirtation with her by mail, but it isn't clear that he ever so much as kissed her.

While Darwin was at Cambridge, prostitutes were available, not to mention the occasional lower-class girl who might settle for less explicit payment. But university proctors prowled the streets near campus, ready to arrest women who could plausibly be accused of "streetwalking." Darwin had been warned by his brother never to be seen with girls. His closest known connection with illicit sex is when he sent money to a friend who had dropped out of school after siring a bastard.[22] Darwin may well have left the shores of England a virgin.[23] And the next five years, spent mainly on a ninety-foot ship with six dozen males, wouldn't provide many opportunities to change that status, at least not through conventional channels.

For that matter, sex wouldn't be abundantly available on his return either. This was, after all, Victorian England. Prostitutes could be had in London (where Darwin would take up residence), but sex with a "respectable" woman, a woman of Darwin's class, was more elusive—close to impossible in the absence of extreme measures, such as marriage.

The great gulf between these two forms of sex is one of the most famous elements of Victorian sexual morality—the "Madonna-whore" dichotomy. There were two kinds of women: the kind a bachelor would later marry and the kind he might now enjoy, the kind worthy of love and the kind that warranted only lust. A second moral attitude commonly traced to the Victorian age is the sexual double standard. Though this attribution is misleading, since Victorian moralists so strongly discouraged sexual license in men *and* women, it's true that a Victorian man's sexual extravagance raised fewer eyebrows than a woman's. It's also true that this distinction was closely linked to the Madonna-whore dichotomy. The great punishment awaiting a sexually adventurous Victorian woman was permanent consignment to the latter half of the dichotomy, which would greatly restrict her range of available husbands.

There is a tendency these days to reject and scoff at these aspects of Victorian morality. Rejecting them is fine, but to scoff at them is to overestimate our own moral advancement. The fact is that many men still speak openly about "sluts" and their proper use: great for recreation, but not for marriage. And even men (such as well-educated liberal ones) who wouldn't dream of talking like that may in fact act like that. Women sometimes complain about seemingly enlightened men who lavish respectful attention on them but then, after sex on the first or second date, never call again, as if early sex had turned the woman into a pariah. Similarly, while the double standard has waned in this century, it is still strong enough for women to complain about. Understanding the Victorian sexual climate can take us some distance toward understanding today's sexual climate.

The intellectual grounding of Victorian sexual morality was explicit: women and men are inherently different, most importantly in the libido department. Even Victorians who railed against male philandering stressed the difference. Dr. Acton wrote: "I should say that the majority of women (happily for them) are not very much troubled with sexual feeling of any kind. What men are habitually, women are only exceptionally. It is too true, I admit, as the divorce courts show, that there are some few women who have sexual desires so strong that they surpass those of men." This "nymphomania" is "a form of insanity." Still, "there can be no doubt that sexual feeling in the female is in the majority of cases in abeyance . . . and even if roused (which in many instances it never can be) is very moderate compared with that of the male." One problem, said Dr. Acton, was that many young men are misled by the sight of "loose or, at least, low and vulgar women." They thus enter marriage with exaggerated notions of its sexual content. They don't understand that "the best mothers, wives, and managers of households, know little or nothing of sexual indulgences. Love of home, children, and domestic duties, are the only passions they feel."[24]

Some women who consider themselves excellent wives and mothers may hold a different opinion. And they may have strong supporting evidence. Still, the idea that there are *some* differences between the typical male and female sexual appetite, and that the male appetite is less finicky, draws much support from the new Darwinian paradigm. For that matter, it draws support from lots of other places. The recently popular premise that men and women are basically identical in nature seems to have fewer and fewer defenders. It is no longer, for example, a cardinal doctrine of feminism. A whole school of feminists—the "difference feminists," or "essentialists"—now accept that men and women are deeply different. What exactly "deeply" means is something they're often vague about, and many would rather not utter the word *genes* in this context. Until they do, they will likely remain in a state of disorientation, aware that the early feminist doctrine of innate sexual symmetry was incorrect (and that it may have in some ways harmed women) yet afraid to honestly explore the alternative.

If the new Darwinian view of sexuality did nothing more than endorse the coalescing conventional wisdom that men are a pretty libidinous group, it would be of meager value. But in fact it sheds light not just on animal impulses, like lust, but on the subtler contours of consciousness. "Sexual psychology," to an evolutionary psychologist, includes everything from an adolescent's fluctuating self-esteem to the aesthetic judgments men and women make about each other to the moral judgments they make about each other, and, for that matter, the moral judgments they make about members of their own sex. Two good examples are the Madonna-whore dichotomy and the sexual double standard. Both now appear to have roots in human nature—in mental mechanisms that people use to evaluate each other.

This calls for a couple of disclaimers. First, to say something is a product of natural selection is not to say that it is unchangeable; just about any manifestation of human nature can be changed, given an apt alteration of the environment—though the required alteration will in some cases be prohibitively drastic. Second, to say that something is "natural" is not to say that it is good. There is no reason to adopt natural selection's "values" as our own. But presumably if we want to pursue values that are at odds with natural selection's, we need to know what we're up against. If we want to change some disconcertingly stubborn parts of our moral code, it would help to know where they come from. And where they *ultimately* come from is human nature, however complexly that nature is refracted by the many layers of circumstance and cultural inheritance through which it passes. No, there is no "double-standard gene." But yes, to understand the double standard we must understand our genes and how

they affect our thoughts. We must understand the process that selected those genes and the strange criteria it used.

We'll spend the next few chapters exploring that process as it
has shaped sexual psychology. Then, thus fortified, we'll return to
Victorian morality, and to Darwin's own mind, and the mind
of the woman he married. All of which will enable us to see our
own situation—courtship and marriage at the end of the twentieth
century—with new clarity.

Chapter 2: **MALE AND FEMALE**

In the most distinct classes of the animal kingdom, with mammals, birds, reptiles, fishes, insects, and even crustaceans, the differences between the sexes follow almost exactly the same rules; the males are almost always the wooers. . . .
— *The Descent of Man* (1871)[1]

Darwin was wrong about sex.

He wasn't wrong about the males being the wooers. His reading of the basic characters of the two sexes holds up well today. "The female, . . . with the rarest exception, is less eager than the male. . . . [S]he is coy, and may often be seen endeavouring for a long time to escape from the male. Every one who has attended to the habits of animals will be able to call to mind instances of this kind. . . . The exertion of some choice on the part of the female seems almost as general a law as the eagerness of the male."[2]

Nor was Darwin wrong about the *consequences* of this asymmetrical interest. He saw that female reticence left males competing with one another for scarce reproductive opportunities, and thus explained why males so often have built-in weapons—the horns of stags, the hornlike mandibles of stag beetles, the fierce canines of chimpanzees.[3] Males not hereditarily equipped for combat with other males have been excluded from sex, and their traits have thus been discarded by natural selection.

Darwin also saw that the choosiness of females gives great moment to their choices. If they prefer to mate with particular kinds of males, those kinds will proliferate. Hence the ornamentation of so many male animals—a lizard's inflatable throat sack, brightly colored during the mating season; the immense, cumbersome tail of the peacock; and, again, the stag's horns, which seem more elaborate than the needs of combat alone would dictate.[4] These decorations have evolved not because they aid in daily survival—if anything, they complicate it—but because they can so charm a female as to outweigh the everyday burdens they bring. (How it came to be in the genetic interest of females to be charmed by such things is another story, and a point of subtle disagreement among biologists.)[5]

Both of these variants of natural selection—combat among males and discernment by females—Darwin called "sexual selection." He took great pride in the idea, and justifiably so. Sexual selection is a nonobvious extension of his general theory that accounts for seeming exceptions to it (like garish colors that virtually say "Kill me" to predators), and that has not just endured over time but grown in scope.

What Darwin was wrong about was the evolutionary *cause* of female coyness and male eagerness. He saw that this imbalance of interest creates competition among males for precious reproductive slots, and he saw the consequences of this competition; but he didn't see what had created the imbalance. His attempt late in life to explain the phenomenon was unsuccessful.[6] And, in fairness to him, whole generations of biologists would do no better.

Now that there is a consensus on the solution, the long failure to find it seems puzzling. It's a very simple solution. In this sense, sex is typical of many behaviors illuminated by natural selection; though the illumination has gotten truly powerful only within the last three decades, it could in principle have done so a century earlier, so plainly does it follow from Darwin's view of life. There is some subtle logic involved, so Darwin can be forgiven for not having seen the full scope of his theory. Still, if he were around today to hear evolutionary biologists talk about sex, he might well sink into one of his self-effacing funks, exclaiming at his obtuseness in not getting the picture sooner.

PLAYING GOD

The first step toward understanding the basic imbalance of the sexes is to assume hypothetically the role natural selection plays in designing a species. Take the human species, for example. Suppose you're in charge of installing, in the minds of human (or prehuman) beings, rules of behavior that will guide them through life, the object of the game being to maximize each person's genetic legacy. To oversimplify a bit: you're supposed to make each person behave in such a way that he or she is likely to have lots of offspring—offspring, moreover, who themselves have lots of offspring.

Obviously, this isn't the way natural selection actually works. It doesn't consciously design organisms. It doesn't consciously do anything. It blindly preserves hereditary traits that happen to enhance survival and reproduction.* Still, natural selection works *as if* it were consciously designing organisms, so pretending you're in charge of organism design is a legitimate way to figure out which tendencies evolution is likely to have ingrained in people and other animals. In fact, this is what evolutionary biologists spend a good deal of time doing: looking at a trait—mental or otherwise—and figuring out what, if any, engineering challenge it is a solution to.

When playing the Administrator of Evolution, and trying to maximize genetic legacy, you quickly discover that this goal implies different tendencies for men and women. Men can reproduce hundreds of times a year, assuming they can persuade enough women to cooperate, and assuming there aren't any laws against polygamy—which there assuredly weren't in the environment where much of our evolution took place. Women, on the other hand, can't reproduce more often than once a year. The asymmetry lies partly in the high price of eggs; in all species they're bigger and rarer than minuscule,

---

*Actually, one premise of the new Darwinian paradigm is that natural selection's guiding light is a bit more complex than "survival and reproduction." But that nuance won't matter until chapter seven.

mass-produced sperm. (That, in fact, is biology's official definition of a female: the one with the larger sex cells.) But the asymmetry is exaggerated by the details of mammalian reproduction; the egg's lengthy conversion into an organism happens inside the female, and she can't handle many projects at once.

So, while there are various reasons why it could make Darwinian sense for a woman to mate with more than one man (maybe the first man was infertile, for example), there comes a time when having more sex just isn't worth the trouble. Better to get some rest or grab a bite to eat. For a man, unless he's really on the brink of collapse or starvation, that time never comes. Each new partner offers a very real chance to get more genes into the next generation—a much more valuable prospect, in the Darwinian calculus, than a nap or a meal. As the evolutionary psychologists Martin Daly and Margo Wilson have succinctly put it: for males "there is always the possibility of doing better."[7]

There's a sense in which a female can do better, too, but it has to do with quality, not quantity. Giving birth to a child involves a huge commitment of time, not to mention energy, and nature has put a low ceiling on how many such enterprises she can undertake. So each child, from her (genetic) point of view, is an extremely precious gene machine. Its ability to survive and then, in turn, produce its own young gene machines is of mammoth importance. It makes Darwinian sense, then, for a woman to be selective about the man who is going to help her build each gene machine. She should size up an aspiring partner before letting him in on the investment, asking herself what he'll bring to the project. This question then entails a number of subquestions that, in the human species especially, are more numerous and subtle than you might guess.

Before we go into these questions, a couple of points must be made. One is that the woman needn't literally ask them, or even be aware of them. Much of the relevant history of our species took place before our ancestors were smart enough to ask much of anything. And even in the more recent past, after the arrival of language and self-awareness, there has been no reason for every evolved behavioral tendency to fall under conscious control. In fact, sometimes it is emphatically *not* in our genetic interest to be aware of exactly what we are doing or why. (Hence Freud, who was definitely onto something, though some evolutionary psychologists would say he didn't know exactly what.) In the case of sexual attraction, at any rate, everyday experience suggests that natural selection has wielded its influence largely via the emotional spigots that turn on and off such feelings as tentative attraction, fierce passion, and swoon-inducing infatuation. A woman doesn't typically size up a man and think: "He seems like a worthy contributor to my genetic legacy." She just sizes him up and feels attracted to him—or doesn't. All the "thinking" has been done—unconsciously, metaphorically—by natural selection. Genes leading to attractions that wound up being good for her ancestors' genetic legacies have flourished, and those leading to less productive attractions have not.

Understanding the often unconscious nature of genetic control is the first step toward understanding that—in many realms, not just sex—we're all puppets, and our best hope for even partial liberation is to try to decipher the logic of the puppeteer. The full scope of the logic will take some time to explain, but I don't think I'm spoiling the end of the movie by noting here that the puppeteer seems to have exactly zero regard for the happiness of the puppets.

The second point to grasp before pondering how natural selection has "decided" to shape the sexual preferences of women (and of men) is that it isn't foresightful. Evolution is guided by the environment in which it takes place, and environments change. Natural selection had no way of anticipating, for example, that someday people would use contraception, and that their passions would thus lead them into time-consuming and energy-sapping sex that was sure to be fruitless; or that X-rated videotapes would come along and lead indiscriminately lustful men to spend leisure time watching them rather than pursuing real, live women who might get their genes to the next generation.

This isn't to say that there's anything wrong with "unproductive" sexual recreation. Just because natural selection created us doesn't mean we have to slavishly follow its peculiar agenda. (If anything, we might be tempted to spite it for all the ridiculous baggage it's saddled us with.) The point is just that it isn't correct to say that people's minds are designed to maximize their fitness, their genetic legacy. What the theory of natural selection says, rather, is that people's minds were designed to maximize fitness *in the environment in which those minds evolved.* This environment is known as the EEA—the environment of evolutionary adaptation.[8] Or, more memorably: the "ancestral environment." Throughout this book, the ancestral environment will lurk in the background. At times, in pondering whether some mental trait is an evolutionary adaptation, I will ask whether it seems to be in the "genetic interest" of its bearer. For example: Would indiscriminate lust be in the genetic interest of men? But this is just a kind of shorthand. The question, properly put, is always whether a trait would be in the "genetic interest" of someone in the EEA, not in modern America or Victorian England or anywhere else. Only traits that would have propelled the genes responsible for them through the generations in our ancestral social environment should, in theory, be part of human nature today.[9]

What was the ancestral environment like? The closest thing to a twentieth-century example is a hunter-gatherer society, such as the !Kung San of the Kalahari Desert in Africa, the Inuit (Eskimos) of the Arctic region, or the Ache of Paraguay. Inconveniently, hunter-gatherer societies are quite different from one another, rendering simple generalization about the crucible of human evolution difficult. This diversity is a reminder that the idea of a single EEA is actually a fiction, a composite drawing; our ancestral social environment no doubt changed much in the course of human evolution.[10] Still, there are recurring themes among contemporary hunter-gatherer societies, and they suggest that some features probably stayed fairly constant during much of the evolution of the human mind. For example: people grew up near close kin in small villages where everyone knew everyone else and strangers didn't show up very often. People got married—monogamously or polygamously—and a female typically was married by the time she was old enough to be fertile.

This much, at any rate, is a safe bet: whatever the ancestral environment was like, it wasn't much like the environment we're in now. We aren't designed to stand on crowded subway platforms, or to live in suburbs next door to people we never talk to, or to get hired or fired, or to watch the evening news. This disjunction between the contexts of our design and of our lives is probably responsible for much psychopathology, as well as much suffering of a less dramatic sort. (And, like the importance of unconscious motivation, it is an observation for which Freud gets some credit; it is central to his *Civilization and Its Discontents*.)

To figure out what women are inclined to seek in a man, and vice versa, we'll need to think more carefully about our ancestral social environment(s). And, as we'll see, thinking about the ancestral environment also helps explain why females in our species are less sexually reserved than females in many other species. But for purposes of making the single, largest point of this chapter—that, whatever the typical level of reserve for females in our species, it is higher than the level for males—the particular environment doesn't much matter. For this point depends only on the premise that an individual female can, over a lifetime, have many fewer offspring than an individual male. And that has been the case, basically, forever: since before our ancestors were human, before they were primates, before they were mammals—way, way back through the evolution of our brain, down to its reptilian core. Female snakes may not be very smart, but they're smart enough to know, unconsciously, at least, that there are some males it's not a good idea to mate with.

Darwin's failure, then, was a failure to see what a deeply precious commodity females are. He saw that their coyness had made them precious, but he didn't see that they were *inherently* precious—precious by virtue of their biological role in reproduction, and the resulting slow rate of female reproduction. Natural selection had seen this—or, at least, had "seen" it—and female coyness is the result of this implicit comprehension.

ENLIGHTENMENT DAWNS

The first large and clear step toward human comprehension of this logic was made in 1948 by the British geneticist A. J. Bateman. Bateman took fruit flies and ran them through a dating game. He would place five males and five females in a chamber, let them follow their hearts, and then, by examining the traits of the next generation, figure out which offspring belonged to which parents. He found a clear pattern. Whereas almost all females had about the same number of offspring, regardless of whether they mated with one, two, or three males, male legacies differed according to a simple rule: the more females you mate with, the more offspring you have. Bateman saw the import: natural selection encourages "an undiscriminating eagerness in the males and a discriminating passivity in the females."[11]

Bateman's insight long lay essentially unappreciated. It took nearly three decades, and several evolutionary biologists, to give it the things it lacked: full and rigorous elaboration on the one hand, and publicity on the other.

The first part—the rigor—came from two biologists who are good examples of how erroneous some stereotypes about Darwinism are. In the 1970s, opposition to sociobiology often took the form of charges that its practitioners were closet reactionaries, racists, fascists, etcetera. It is hard to imagine two people less vulnerable to such charges than George Williams and Robert Trivers, and it is hard to name anyone who did more than they to lay the foundations of the new paradigm.

Williams, a professor emeritus at the State University of New York, has worked hard to dispel vestiges of social Darwinism, with its underlying assumption that natural selection is a process somehow worthy of obedience or emulation. Many biologists share his view, and stress that we can't derive our moral values from its "values." But Williams goes further. Natural selection, he says, is an "evil" process, so great is the pain and death it thrives on, so deep is the selfishness it engenders.

Trivers, who was an untenured professor at Harvard when the new paradigm was taking shape and is now at Rutgers University, is much less inclined than Williams toward moral philosophy. But he evinces an emphatic failure to buy the right-wing values associated with social Darwinism. He speaks proudly of his friendship with the late Black Panther leader Huey Newton (with whom he once co-authored an article on human psychology). He rails against the bias of the judicial system. He sees conservative conspiracies where some people don't.

In 1966 Williams published his landmark work, *Adaptation and Natural Selection: A Critique of Some Current Evolutionary Thought.*

Slowly this book has acquired a nearly holy stature in its field. It is a basic text for biologists who think about social behavior, including human social behavior, in light of the new Darwinism.[12] Williams's book dispelled confusions that had long plagued the study of social behavior, and it laid down foundational insights that would support whole edifices of work on the subjects of friendship and sex. In both cases Trivers would be instrumental in building the edifices.

Williams amplified and extended the logic behind Bateman's 1948 paper. He cast the issue of male versus female genetic interests in terms of the "sacrifice" required for reproduction. For a male mammal, the necessary sacrifice is close to zero. His "essential role may end with copulation, which involves a negligible expenditure of energy and materials on his part, and only a momentary lapse of attention from matters of direct concern to his safety and well-being." With little to lose and much to gain, males can profit, in the currency of natural selection, by harboring "an aggressive and immediate willingness to mate with as many females as may be available." For the female, on the other hand, "copulation may mean a commitment to a prolonged burden, in both the mechanical and physiological sense, and its many attendant stresses and dangers." Thus, it is in her genetic interest to "assume the burdens of reproduction" only when circumstances seem propitious. And "one of the most important circumstances is the inseminating male"; since "unusually fit fathers tend to have unusually fit offspring," it is "to the female's advantage to be able to pick the most fit male available. . . . "[13]

Hence courtship: "the advertisement, by a male, of how fit he is." And just as "it is to his advantage to pretend to be highly fit whether he is or not," it is to the female's advantage to spot false advertising. So natural selection creates "a skilled salesmanship among the males and an equally well-developed sales resistance and discrimination among the females."[14] In other words: males should, in theory, tend to be show-offs.

A few years later, Trivers used the ideas of Bateman and Williams to create a full-blown theory that ever since has been shedding light on the psychology of men and women. Trivers began by replacing Williams's concept of "sacrifice" with "investment." The difference may seem slight, but nuances can start intellectual avalanches, and this one did. The term *investment*, linked to economics, comes with a ready-made analytical framework.

In a now-famous paper published in 1972, Trivers formally defined "parental investment" as "any investment by the parent in an individual offspring that increases the offspring's chance of surviving (and hence [the offspring's] reproductive success) at the cost of the parent's ability to invest in other offspring."[15] Parental investment includes the time and energy consumed in producing an egg or a sperm, achieving fertilization, gestating or incubating the egg, and rearing the offspring. Plainly, females will generally make the higher investment up until birth, and, less plainly but in fact typically, this disparity continues after birth.

By quantifying the imbalance of investment between mother and father in a given species, Trivers suggested, we could better understand many things—for example, the extent of male eagerness and female coyness, the intensity of sexual selection, and many subtle aspects of courtship and parenthood, fidelity and infidelity. Trivers saw that in our species the imbalance of investment is not as stark as in many others. And he correctly suspected that (as we'll see in the next chapter) the result is much psychological complexity.

At last, with Trivers's paper "Parental Investment and Sexual Selection," the flower had bloomed; a simple extension of Darwin's theory—so simple that Darwin would have grasped it in a minute—had been glimpsed in 1948, clearly articulated in 1966, and was now, in 1972, given full form.[16] Still, the concept of parental investment lacked one thing: publicity. It was E. O. Wilson's book *Sociobiology* (1975) and Richard Dawkins's *The Selfish Gene* (1976) that gave Trivers's work a large and diverse audience, getting scores of psychologists and anthropologists to think about human sexuality in modern Darwinian terms. The resulting insights are likely to keep accumulating for a long time.

TESTING THE THEORY

Theories are a dime a dozen. Even strikingly elegant theories, which, like the theory of parental investment, seem able to explain much with little, often turn out to be worthless. There is justice in the complaint (from creationists, among others) that some theories about the evolution of animal traits are "just so stories"—plausible, but nothing more. Still, it is possible to separate the merely plausible from the compelling. In some sciences, testing theories is so straightforward that it is only a slight exaggeration (though it is always, in a certain strict sense, an exaggeration) to talk of theories being "proved." In others, corroboration is roundabout—an ongoing, gradual process by which confidence approaches the threshold of consensus, or fails to. Studying the evolutionary roots of human nature, or of anything else, is a science of the second sort. About each theory we ask a series of questions, and the answers nourish belief or doubt or ambivalence.

One question about the theory of parental investment is whether human behavior in fact complies with it in even the most basic ways. Are women more choosy about sex partners than men? (This is not to be confused with the very different question, to which we'll return, of which sex, if either, is choosier about *marriage* partners.) Certainly there is plenty of folk wisdom suggesting as much. More concretely, there's the fact that prostitution—sex with someone you don't know and don't care to know—is a service sought overwhelmingly by males, now as in Victorian England. Similarly, virtually all pornography that relies sheerly on visual stimulation—pictures or films of anonymous people, spiritless flesh—is consumed by males. And various studies have shown men to be, on average, much more open to casual, anonymous sex than women. In one experiment, three fourths of the men approached by an unknown woman on a college campus agreed to have sex with her, whereas none of the women approached by an unknown man were willing.[17]

It used to be common for doubters to complain that this sort of evidence, drawn from Western society, reflects only its warped values. This tack has been problematic since 1979, when Donald Symons published *The Evolution of Human Sexuality,* the first comprehensive anthropological survey of human sexual behavior from the new Darwinian perspective. Drawing on cultures East and West, industrial and preliterate, Symons demonstrated the great breadth of the patterns implied by the theory of parental investment: women tend to be relatively selective about sex partners; men tend to be less so, and tend to find sex with a wide variety of partners an extraordinarily appealing concept.

One culture Symons discussed is about as far from Western influence as possible: the indigenous culture of the Trobriand Islands in Melanesia. The prehistoric migration that populated these islands broke off from the migrations that peopled Europe at least tens of thousands of years ago, and possibly more than 100,000 years ago. The Trobrianders' ancestral culture was separated from Europe's ancestral culture even earlier than was that of Native Americans.[18] And indeed, when visited by the great anthropologist Bronislaw Malinowski in 1915, the islands proved startlingly remote from the currents of Western thought. The natives, it seemed, hadn't even gotten the connection between sex and reproduction. When one seafaring Trobriander returned from a voyage of several years to find his wife with two children, Malinowski was tactful enough not to suggest that she had been unfaithful. And "when I discussed the matter with others, suggesting that one at least of these children could not be his, my interlocutors did not understand what I meant."[19]

Some anthropologists have doubted that the Trobrianders could have been so ignorant. And although Malinowski's account of this issue seems to have the ring of authority, there is no way of knowing whether he got the story straight. But it is important to understand that he could, in principle, be right. The evolution of human sexual psychology seems to have preceded the discovery by humans of what sex is for. Lust and other such feelings are natural selection's way of getting us to act as if we wanted lots of offspring and knew how to get them, whether or not we actually do.[20] Had natural selection *not* worked this way—had it instead harnessed human intelligence so that our pursuit of fitness was entirely conscious and calculated—then life would be very different. Husbands and wives would, for example, spend no time having extramarital affairs with contraception; they would either scrap the contraception or scrap the sex.

Another un-Western thing about Trobriand culture was the lack of Victorian anxiety about premarital sex. By early adolescence, both girls and boys were encouraged to mate with a series of partners to their liking. (This freedom is found in some other preindustrial societies, though the experimentation typically ends, and marriage begins, before a girl reaches fertility.) But Malinowski left no doubt about which sex was choosier. "[T]here is nothing roundabout in a Trobriand wooing. . . . Simply and directly a meeting is asked for with the avowed intention of sexual gratification. If the invitation is accepted, the satisfaction of the boy's desire eliminates the romantic frame of mind, the craving for the unattainable and mysterious. If he is rejected, there is not much room for personal tragedy, for he is accustomed from childhood to having his sexual impulses thwarted by some girl, and he knows that another intrigue cures this type of ill surely and swiftly. . . . " And: "In the course of every love affair the man has constantly to give small presents to the woman. To the natives the need of one-sided payment is self-evident. This custom implies that sexual intercourse, even where there is mutual attachment, is a service rendered by the female to the male."[21]

There were certainly cultural forces reinforcing coyness among Trobriand women. Though a young woman was encouraged to have an active sex life, her advances would be frowned on if too overt and common because of the "small sense of personal worth that such urgent solicitation implies."[22] But is there any reason to believe this norm was anything other than a culturally mediated reflection of deeper genetic logic? Can anyone find a single culture in which women with unrestrained sexual appetites *aren't* viewed as more aberrant than comparably libidinous men? If not, isn't it an astonishing coincidence that all peoples have independently arrived at roughly the same cultural destination, with no genetic encouragement? Or is it the case that this universal cultural element was present half a million or more years ago, before the species began splitting up? That seems a long time for an essentially arbitrary value to endure, without being extinguished in a single culture.

This exercise holds a couple of important lessons. First: one good reason to suspect an evolutionary explanation for something—some mental trait or mechanism of mental development—is that it's universal, found everywhere, even in cultures that are as far apart as two cultures can be.[23] Second: the general difficulty of explaining such universality in utterly cultural terms is an example of how the Darwinian view, though not *proved* right in the sense that mathematical theorems are proved right, can still be the view that, by the rules of science, wins; its chain of explanation is shorter than the alternative chain and has fewer dubious links; it is a simpler and more potent theory. If we accept even the three meager assertions made so far— (1) that the theory of natural selection straightforwardly implies the "fitness" of women who are choosy about sexual partners and of men who often aren't; (2) that this choosiness and unchoosiness, respectively, is observed worldwide; and (3) that this universality can't be explained with equal simplicity by a competing, purely cultural, theory—if we accept these things, and if we're playing by the rules of science, we have to endorse the Darwinian explanation: male license and (relative) female reserve are to some extent innate.

Still, it is always good to have more evidence. Though absolute "proof" may not be possible in science, varying degrees of confidence are. And while evolutionary explanations rarely attain the 99.99 percent confidence sometimes found in physics or chemistry, it's always nice to raise the level from, say, 70 to 97 percent.

One way to strengthen an evolutionary explanation is to show that its logic is obeyed generally. If women are choosy about sex because they can have fewer kids than men (by virtue of investing more in them), and if females in the animal kingdom generally can have fewer offspring than males, then female animals in general should be choosier than males. Evolutionary theories can generate falsifiable predictions, as good scientific theories are expected to do, even though evolutionary biologists don't have the luxury of rerunning evolution in their labs, with some of its variables controlled, and predicting the outcome.

This particular prediction has been abundantly confirmed. In species after species, females are coy and males are not. Indeed, males are so dim in their sexual discernment that they may pursue things other than females. Among some kinds of frogs, mistaken homosexual courtship is so common that a "release call" is used by males who find themselves in the clutches of another male to notify him that they're both wasting their time.[24] Male snakes, for their part, have been known to spend a while with dead females before moving on to a live prospect.[25] And male turkeys will avidly court a stuffed replica of a female turkey. In fact, a replica of a female turkey's head suspended fifteen inches from the ground will generally do the trick. The male circles the head, does its ritual displays, and then (confident, presumably, that its performance has been impressive) rises into the air and comes down in the proximity of the female's backside, which turns out not to exist. The more virile males will show such interest even when a wooden head is used, and a few can summon lust for a wooden head with no eyes or beak.[26]

Of course, such experiments only confirm in vivid form what Darwin had much earlier said was obvious: males are very eager. This raises a much-cited problem with testing evolutionary explanations: the odd sense in which a theory's "predictions" are confirmed. Darwin didn't sit in his study and say, "My theory implies coy, picky females and mindlessly lustful males," and then take a walk to see if he could find examples. On the contrary, the many examples are what prompted him to wonder which implication of natural selection had created them—a question not correctly answered until midway through the following century, after even more examples had piled up. This tendency for Darwinian "predictions" to come after their evident fulfillment has been a chronic gripe of Darwin's critics. People who doubt the theory of natural selection, or just resist its application to human behavior, complain about the retrofitting of fresh predictions to preexisting results. This is often what they have in mind when they say evolutionary biologists spend their time dreaming up "just so stories" to explain everything they see.

In a sense, dreaming up plausible stories *is* what evolutionary biologists do. But that's not by itself a damning indictment. The power of a theory, such as the theory of parental investment, is gauged by how much data it explains and how simply, regardless of when the data surfaced. After Copernicus showed that assuming the Earth to revolve around the Sun accounted elegantly for the otherwise perplexing patterns that stars trace in the sky, it would have been beside the point to say, "But you cheated. You knew about the patterns all along." Some "just so stories" are plainly better than others, and they win. Besides, how much choice do evolutionary biologists have? There's not much they can do about the fact that the database on animal life began accumulating millennia before Darwin's theory.

But there is one thing they can do. Often a Darwinian theory generates, in addition to the pseudopredictions that the theory was in fact designed to explain, additional predictions—real predictions, untested predictions, which can be used to further evaluate the theory. (Darwin elliptically outlined this method in 1838, at age twenty-nine—more than twenty years before *The Origin of Species* was published. He wrote in his notebook: "The line of argument pursued throughout my theory is to establish a point as a probability by induction, & to apply it as hypothesis to other points. & see whether it will solve them.")[27] The theory of parental investment is a good example. For there are a few oddball species, as Williams noted in 1966, in which the male's investment in the offspring roughly matches, or even exceeds, the female's. If the theory of parental investment is right, these species should defy sex stereotypes.

Consider seahorses, and their near relative, the pipefish. Here the male plays a role like a female kangaroo's: he takes the eggs into a pouch and plugs them into his bloodstream for nutrition. The female can thus start on another round of reproduction while the male is playing nurse. This may not mean that she can have more offspring than he over a lifetime—after all, it took her a while to produce the eggs in the first place. Still, the parental investment isn't grossly imbalanced in the usual direction. And, predictably, female pipefish and seahorses tend to take an active role in courtship, seeking out the males and initiating the mating ritual.[28]

Some birds, such as the phalarope (including the two species known as sea snipes), exhibit a similarly abnormal distribution of parental investment. The males sit on the eggs, leaving the females free to go get some wild oats sown. Again, we see the expected departure from stereotype. It is the phalarope *females* who are larger and more colorful—a sign that sexual selection is working in reverse, as females compete for males. One biologist observed that the females, in classically male fashion, "quarrel and display among themselves" while the males patiently incubate the eggs.[29]

If the truth be told, Williams knew that these species defy stereotype when he wrote in 1966. But subsequent investigation has confirmed his "prediction" more broadly. Extensive parental investment by males has been shown to have the expected consequences in other birds, in the Panamanian poison-arrow frog, in a water bug whose males cart fertilized eggs around on their backs, and in the (ironically named, it turns out) Mormon cricket. So far Williams's prediction has encountered no serious trouble.[30]

APES AND US

There is another major form of evolutionary evidence bearing on differences between men and women: our nearest relatives. The great apes—chimpanzees, pygmy chimps (also called bonobos), gorillas, and orangutans—are not, of course, our ancestors; all have evolved since their path diverged from ours. Still, those forks in the road have come between eight million years ago (for chimps and bonobos) and sixteen million years ago (for orangutans).[31] That's not long, as these things go. (A reference point: The australopithecine, our presumed ancestor, whose skull was ape-sized but who walked upright, appeared between six and four million years ago, shortly after the chimpanzee off-ramp. *Homo erectus*—the species that had brains midway in size between ours and apes', and used them to discover fire—took shape around 1.5 million years ago.)[32]

The great apes' nearness to us on the evolutionary tree legitimizes a kind of detective game. It's possible—though hardly certain—that when a trait is shared by all of them and by us, the reason is common descent. In other words: the trait existed in our common, sixteen-million-year-old proto-ape ancestor, and has been in all our lineages ever since. The logic is roughly the same as tracking down four distant cousins, finding that they all have brown eyes, and inferring that at least one of their two common great-great-grandparents had brown eyes. It's far from being an airtight conclusion, but it has more credence than it had when you had seen only one of the cousins.[33]

Lots of traits are shared by us and the great apes. For many of the traits—five-fingered hands, say—pointing this out isn't worth the trouble; no one doubts the genetic basis of human hands anyway. But in the case of human mental traits whose genetic substratum is still debated—such as the differing sexual appetites of men and women—this inter-ape comparison can be useful. Besides, it's worth taking a minute to get acquainted with our nearest relatives. Who knows how much of our psyche we share by common descent with some or all of them?

Orangutan males are drifters. They wander in solitude, looking for females, who tend to be stationary, each in her own home range. A male may settle down long enough to monopolize one, two, or even more of these ranges, though vast monopolies are discouraged by the attendant need to fend off vast numbers of rivals. Once the mission is accomplished, and the resident female gives birth, the male is likely to disappear. He may return years later, when pregnai.cy is again possible.[34] In the meantime, he doesn't bother to write.

For a gorilla male, the goal is to become leader of a pack comprising several adult females, their young offspring, and maybe a few young adult males. As dominant male, he will get sole sexual access to the females; the young males generally mind their manners (though a leader may, as he ages and his strength ebbs, share females with them).[35] On the downside, the leader does have to confront any male interlopers, each of which aims to make off with one or more of his females and thus is in an assertive mood.

The life of the male chimpanzee is also combative. He strives to climb a male hierarchy that is long and fluid compared to a gorilla hierarchy. And, again, the dominant male—working tirelessly to protect his rank through assault, intimidation, and cunning—gets first dibs on any females, a prerogative he enforces with special vigor when they're ovulating.[36]

Pygmy chimps, or bonobos (they're actually a distinct species from chimpanzees), may be the most erotic of all primates. Their sex comes in many forms and often serves purposes other than reproduction. Periodic homosexual behavior, such as genital rubbings between females, seems to be a way of saying, "Let's be friends." Still, broadly speaking, the bonobos' sociosexual outline mirrors that of the common chimpanzees: a pronounced male hierarchy that helps determine access to females.[37]

Amid the great variety of social structure in these species, the basic theme of this chapter stands out, at least in minimal form: males seem very eager for sex and work hard to find it; females work less hard. This isn't to say the females don't like sex. They love it, and may initiate it. And, intriguingly, the females of the species most closely related to humans—chimpanzees and bonobos—seem particularly amenable to a wild sex life, including a variety of partners. Still, female apes don't do what male apes do: search high and low, risking life and limb, to find sex, and to find as much of it, with as many different partners, as possible; it has a way of finding them.

FEMALE CHOICE

That female apes are, on balance, more reticent than male apes doesn't necessarily mean that they actively screen their prospective partners. To be sure, the partners get screened; those who dominate other males mate, while those who get dominated may not. This competition is exactly what Darwin had in mind in defining one of the two kinds of sexual selection, and these species (like our own) illustrate how it favors the evolution of big, mean males. But what about the other kind of sexual selection? Does the female participate in the screening, choosing the male that seems the most auspicious contributor to her project?

Female choice is notoriously hard to spot, and signs of its long-term effect are often ambiguous. Are males larger and stronger than females just because tougher males have bested their rivals and gotten to mate? Or, in addition, have females come to prefer tough males, since females with this genetically ingrained preference have had tougher and therefore more prolific sons, whose many daughters then inherited their grandmother's taste?

Notwithstanding such difficulties, it's fairly safe to say that in one sense or another, females are choosy in all the great ape species. A female gorilla, for example, though generally confined to sex with a single, dominant male, normally emigrates in the course of her lifetime. When an alien male approaches her pack, engaging its leader in mutual threats and maybe even a fight, she will, if sufficiently impressed, decide to follow him.[38]

In the case of chimps, the matter is more subtle. The dominant, or alpha, male can have any female he wants, but that's not necessarily because she prefers him; he shuts off alternatives by frightening other males. He can frighten her too, so that any spurning of low-ranking males may reflect only her fear. (Indeed, the spurning has been known to disappear when the alpha isn't looking.)[39] But there is a wholly different kind of chimp mating—a sustained, private consortship that may be a prototype for human courtship. A male and female chimp will leave the community for days or even weeks. And although the female may be forcibly abducted if she resists an invitation, there are times when she successfully resists, and times when she chooses to go peacefully, even though nearby males would gladly aid her in any resistance.[40]

Actually, even going unpeacefully can involve a kind of choice. Female orangutans are a good example. They do often seem to exercise positive choice, favoring some males over others. But sometimes they resist a mating and are forcibly subdued and—insofar as this word can be applied to nonhumans—raped. There is evidence that the rapists, often adolescents, usually fail to impregnate.[41] But suppose that they succeed with some regularity. Then a female, in sheerly Darwinian terms, is better off mating with a good rapist, a big, strong, sexually aggressive male; her male offspring will then be more likely to be big, strong, and sexually aggressive (assuming sexual aggressiveness varies at least in part because of genetic differences)—and therefore prolific. So female resistance should be favored by natural selection as a way to avoid having a son who is an inept rapist (assuming it doesn't bring injury to the female).

This isn't to say that a female primate, her protests notwithstanding, "really wants it," as human males have been known to assume. On the contrary, the more an orangutan "really wants it," the less she'll resist, and the less powerful a screening device her reticence will be. What natural selection "wants" and what any individual wants needn't be the same, and in this case they're somewhat at odds. The point is simply that, even when females demonstrate no clear preference for certain kinds of males, they may be, in practical terms, preferring a certain kind of male. And this de facto discretion may be de jure. It may be an adaptation, favored by natural selection precisely *because* it has this filtering effect.

In the broadest sense, the same logic could apply in any primate species. Once females in general begin putting up the slightest resistance, then a female that puts up a little extra resistance is exhibiting a valuable trait. For whatever it takes to penetrate resistance, the sons of strong resisters are more likely to have it than the sons of weak resisters. (This assumes, again, that the relative possession by different males of "whatever it takes" reflects underlying genetic differences.) Thus, in sheerly Darwinian terms, coyness becomes its own reward. And this is true regardless of whether the male's means of approach is physical or verbal.

ANIMALS AND THE UNCONSCIOUS

A common reaction to the new Darwinian view of sex is that it makes perfect sense as an explanation for animal behavior—which is to say, for the behavior of *nonhuman* animals. People may chuckle appreciatively at a male turkey that tries to mate with a poor rendition of a female's head, but if you then point out that many a human male regularly gets aroused after looking at two-dimensional representations of a nude woman, they don't see the connection. After all, the man surely knows that it's only a photo he's looking at; his behavior may be pathetic, but it isn't comic.

And maybe it isn't. But if he "knows" it's a photo, why is he getting so excited? And why are women so seldom whipped up into an onanistic frenzy by pictures of men?

Resistance to lumping humans and turkeys under one set of Darwinian rules has its points. Yes, our behavior is under more subtle, presumably more "conscious," control than is turkey behavior. Men can decide not to get aroused by something—or, at least, can decide not to look at something they know will arouse them. Sometimes they even stick with those decisions. And although turkeys can make what look like comparable "choices" (a turkey hounded by a shotgun-wielding man may decide that now isn't the time for romance), it is plainly true that the complexity and subtlety of options available to a human are unrivaled in the animal kingdom. So too is the human's considered pursuit of very long-run goals.

It all feels very rational, and in some ways it is. But that doesn't mean it isn't in the service of Darwinian ends. To a layperson, it may seem natural that the evolution of reflective, self-conscious brains would liberate us from the base dictates of our evolutionary past. To an evolutionary biologist, what seems natural is roughly the opposite: that human brains evolved not to insulate us from the mandate to survive and reproduce, but to follow it more effectively, if more pliably; that as we evolve from a species whose males forcibly abduct females into a species whose males whisper sweet nothings, the whispering will be governed by the same logic as the abduction—it is a means of manipulating females to male ends, and its form serves this function. The basic emanations of natural selection are refracted from the older, inner parts of our brain all the way out to its freshest tissue. Indeed, the freshest tissue would never have appeared if it didn't toe natural selection's bottom line.

Of course, a lot *has* happened since our ancestors parted ways with the great apes' ancestors, and one can imagine a change in evolutionary context that would have removed our lineage from the logic that so imbalances the romantic interests of male and female in most species. Don't forget about the seahorses, sea snipes, Panamanian poison-arrow frogs, and Mormon crickets, with their reversed sex roles. And, less dramatically, but a bit closer to home, there are the gibbons, another of our primate cousins, whose ancestors waved good-bye to ours about twenty million years ago. At some point in gibbon evolution, circumstances began to encourage much male parental investment. The males regularly stick around and help provide for the kids. In one gibbon species the males actually carry the infants, something male apes aren't exactly known for. And talk about marital harmony: gibbon couples sing a loud duet in the morning, pointedly advertising their familial stability for the information of would-be home-wreckers.[42]

Well, human males too have been known to carry around infants, and to stay with their families. Is it possible that at some time over the last few million years something happened to us rather like what happened to the gibbons? Have male and female sexual appetites converged at least enough to make monogamous marriage a reasonable goal?

Chapter 3: **MEN AND WOMEN**

Judging from the social habits of man as he now exists, and from most savages being polygamists, the most probable view is that primeval man aboriginally lived in small communities, each with as many wives as he could support and obtain, whom he would have jealously guarded against all other men. Or he may have lived with several wives by himself, like the Gorilla. . . .

—The Descent of Man (1871)[1]

One of the more upbeat ideas to have emerged from an evolutionary view of sex is that human beings are a "pair-bonding" species. In its most extreme form, the claim is that men and women are designed for a lifetime of deep, monogamous love. This claim has not emerged from close scrutiny in pristine condition.

The pair-bond hypothesis was popularized by Desmond Morris in his 1967 book *The Naked Ape*. This book, along with a few other 1960s books (Robert Ardrey's *The Territorial Imperative*, for example), represent a would-be watershed in the history of evolutionary thought. That they found large readerships signaled a new openness to Darwinism, an encouraging dissipation of the fallout from its past political misuses. But there was no way, in the end, that these books could start a Darwinian renaissance within academia. The problem was simple: they didn't make sense.

One example surfaced early in Morris's pair-bonding argument. He was trying to explain why human females are generally faithful to their mates. This is indeed a good question (if you believe they are, that is). For high fidelity would place women in a distinct minority within the animal kingdom. Though female animals are generally less licentious than males, the females of many species are far from prudes, and this is particularly true of our nearest ape relatives. Female chimpanzees and bonobos are, at times, veritable sex machines. In explaining how women came to be so virtuous, Morris referred to the sexual division of labor in an early hunter-gatherer economy. "To begin with," he wrote, "the males had to be sure that their females were going to be faithful to them when they left them alone to go hunting. So the females had to develop a pairing tendency."[2]

Stop right there. It was in the reproductive interests of the *males* for the *females* to develop a tendency toward fidelity? So natural selection obliged the males by making the necessary changes in the females? Morris never got around to explaining how, exactly, natural selection would perform this generous feat.

Maybe it's unfair to single Morris out for blame. He was a victim of his times. The trouble was an atmosphere of loose, hyperteleological thinking. One gets the impression, reading Morris's book, and Ardrey's books, of a natural selection that peers into the future, decides what needs to be done to make things generally better for the species, and takes the necessary steps. But natural selection doesn't work that way. It doesn't peer ahead, and it doesn't try to make things generally better. Every single, tiny, blindly taken step either happens to make sense in immediate terms of genetic self-interest or it doesn't. And if it doesn't, you won't be reading about it a million years later. This was an essential message of George Williams's 1966 book, a message that had barely begun to take hold when Morris's book appeared.

One key to good evolutionary analysis, Williams stressed, is to focus on the fate of the gene in question. If a woman's "fidelity gene" (or her "infidelity gene") shapes her behavior in a way that helps get copies of *itself* into future generations in large numbers, then that gene will by definition flourish. Whether the gene, in the process, gets mixed in with her husband's genes or with the mailman's genes is by itself irrelevant. As far as natural selection is concerned, one vehicle is as good as the next. (Of course, when we talk about "a gene" for anything—fidelity, infidelity, altruism, cruelty—we are usefully oversimplifying; complex traits result from the interaction of numerous genes, each of which, typically, was selected for its incremental addition to fitness.)

A new wave of evolutionists has used this stricter view of natural selection to think with greater care about the question that rightly interested Morris: Are human males and females born to form enduring bonds with one another? The answer is hardly an unqualified yes for either sex. Still, it is closer to a yes for both sexes than it is in the case of, say, chimpanzees. In every human culture on the anthropological record, marriage—whether monogamous or polygamous, permanent or temporary—is the norm, and the family is the atom of social organization. Fathers everywhere feel love for their children, and that's a lot more than you can say for chimp fathers and bonobo fathers, who don't seem to have much of a clue as to which youngsters are theirs. This love leads fathers to help feed and defend their children, and teach them useful things.[3]

At some point, in other words, extensive *male parental investment* entered our evolutionary lineage. We are, as they say in the zoology literature, high in MPI. We're not so high that male parental investment typically rivals female parental investment, but we're a lot higher than the average primate. We indeed have something important in common with the gibbons.

High MPI has in some ways made the everyday goals of male and female humans dovetail, and, as any two parents know, it can give them a periodic source of common and profound joy. But high MPI has also created whole new ways for male and female aims to diverge, during both courtship and marriage. In Robert Trivers's 1972 paper on parental investment, he remarked, "One can, in effect, treat the sexes as if they were different species, the opposite sex being a resource relevant to producing maximum surviving offspring."[4] Trivers was making a specific analytical point, not a sweeping rhetorical one. But to a distressing extent—and an extent that was unclear before his paper—this metaphor does capture the overall situation; even with high MPI, and in some ways because of it, a basic underlying dynamic between men and women is mutual exploitation. They seem, at times, designed to make each other miserable.

WHY WE'RE HIGH IN MPI

There is no shortage of clues as to why men are inclined to help rear their young. In our recent evolutionary past lie several factors that can make parental investment worthwhile from the point of view of the male's genes.[5] In other words, because of these factors, genes inclining a male to love his offspring—to worry about them, defend them, provide for them, educate them—could flourish at the expense of genes that counseled continued remoteness.

One factor is the vulnerability of offspring. Following the generic male sexual strategy—roaming around, seducing and abandoning everything in sight—won't do a male's genes much good if the resulting offspring get eaten. That seems to be one reason so many bird species are monogamous, or at least relatively monogamous. Eggs left alone while the mother went out and hunted worms wouldn't last long. When our ancestors moved from the forests out onto the savanna, they had to cope with fleet predators. And this was hardly the only new danger to the young. As the species got smarter and its posture more upright, female anatomy faced a paradox: walking upright implied a narrow pelvis, and thus a narrow birth canal, but the heads of babies were larger than ever. This is presumably why human infants are born prematurely in comparison to other primates. From early on, baby chimps can cling to their mother while she walks around, her hands unencumbered. Human babies, though, seriously compromise a mother's food gathering. For many months, they're mounds of helpless flesh: tiger bait.

Meanwhile, as the genetic payoff of male investment was growing, the cost of investment was dropping. Hunting seems to have figured heavily in our evolution. With men securing handy, dense packages of protein, feeding a family was practical. It is probably no coincidence that monogamy is more common among carnivorous mammals than among vegetarians.

On top of all of this, as the human brain got bigger, it probably depended more on early cultural programming. Children with two parents may have had an educational edge over children with only one.

Characteristically, natural selection appears to have taken this cost-benefit calculus and transmuted it into feeling—in particular, the sensation of love. And not just love for the *child;* the first step toward becoming a solid parental unit is for the man and woman to develop a strong mutual attraction. The genetic payoff of having two parents devoted to a child's welfare is the reason men and women can fall into swoons over one another, including swoons of great duration.

Until recently, this claim was heresy. "Romantic love" was thought to be an invention of Western culture; there were reports of cultures in which choice of mate had nothing to do with affection, and sex carried no emotional weight. But lately anthropologists mindful of the Darwinian logic behind attachment have taken a second look, and such reports are falling into doubt.[6] Love between man and woman appears to have an innate basis. In this sense, the "pair-bonding" hypothesis stands supported, though not for all the reasons Desmond Morris imagined.

At the same time, the term *pair bonding*—and for that matter, the term *love*—conveys a sense of permanence and symmetry that, as any casual observer of our species can see, is not always warranted. To fully appreciate how large is the gap between idealized love and the version of love natural to people, we need to do what Trivers did in his 1972 paper: focus not on the emotion itself, but on the abstract evolutionary logic it embodies. What are the respective genetic interests of males and females in a species with internal fertilization, an extended period of gestation, prolonged infant dependence on mother's milk, and fairly high male parental investment? Seeing these interests clearly is the only way to appreciate how evolution not only invented romantic love, but, from the beginning, corrupted it.

WHAT DO WOMEN WANT?

For a species low in male parental investment, the basic dynamic of courtship, as we've seen, is pretty simple: the male really wants sex; the female isn't so sure.[7] She may want time to (unconsciously) assess the quality of his genes, whether by inspecting him or by letting him battle with other males for her favor. She may also pause to weigh the chances that he carries disease. And she may try to extract a precopulation gift, taking advantage of the high demand for her eggs. This "nuptial offering"—which technically constitutes a tiny male parental investment, since it nourishes her and her eggs—is seen in a variety of species, ranging from primates to black-tipped hanging flies. (The female hanging fly insists on having a dead insect to eat during sex. If she finishes it before the male is finished, she may head off in search of another meal, leaving him high and dry. If she isn't so quick, the male may repossess the leftovers for subsequent dates.)[8] These various female concerns can usually be addressed fairly quickly; there's no reason for courtship to drag on for weeks.

But now throw high MPI into the equation—male investment not just at the time of sex, but extending up to and well beyond birth. Suddenly the female is concerned not only with the male's genetic investment, or with a free meal, but with what he'll bring to the offspring after it materializes. In 1989 the evolutionary psychologist David Buss published a pioneering study of mate preferences in thirty-seven cultures around the world. He found that in every culture, females placed more emphasis than males on a potential mate's financial prospects.[9]

That doesn't mean women have a specific, evolved preference for *wealthy* men. Most hunter-gatherer societies have very little in the way of accumulated resources and private property. Whether this accurately reflects the ancestral environment is controversial; hunter-gatherers have, over the last few millennia, been shoved off of rich land into marginal habitats and thus may not, in this respect, be representative of our ancestors. But if indeed all men in the ancestral environment were about equally affluent (that is, not very), women may be innately attuned not so much to a man's wealth as to his social status; among hunter-gatherers, status often translates into power—influence over the divvying up of resources, such as meat after a big kill. In modern societies, in any event, wealth, status, and power often go hand in hand, and seem to make an attractive package in the eyes of the average woman.

Ambition and industry also seem to strike many women as aus-

picious—and Buss found that this pattern, too, is broadly interna-
tional.[10] Of course, ambition and industriousness are things a female
might look for even in a low-MPI species, as indices of genetic quality.
Not so, however, for her assessment of the male's *willingness* to
invest. A female in a high-MPI species may seek signs of generosity,
trustworthiness, and, especially, an enduring commitment to her in
particular. It is a truism that flowers and other tokens of affection
are more prized by women than by men.

Why should women be so suspicious of men? After all, aren't
males in a high-MPI species designed to settle down, buy a house,
and mow the lawn every weekend? Here arises the first problem with
terms like *love* and *pair bonding*. Males in high-MPI species are,
paradoxically, capable of greater treachery than males in low-MPI
species. For the "optimal male course," as Trivers noted, is a "mixed
strategy."[11] Even if long-term investment is their main aim, seduction
and abandonment can make genetic sense, provided it doesn't take
too much, in time and other resources, from the offspring in which
the male *does* invest. The bastard youngsters may thrive even without
paternal investment; they may, for that matter, attract investment
from some poor sap who is under the impression that they're his. So
males in a high-MPI species should, in theory, be ever alert for
opportunistic sex.

Of course, so should males in a low-MPI species. But this doesn't
amount to exploitation, since the female has no chance of getting
much more from another male. In a high-MPI species, she does, and
a failure to get it from any male can be quite costly.

The result of these conflicting aims—the female aversion to exploitation, the male affinity for exploiting—is an evolutionary arms
race. Natural selection may favor males that are good at deceiving
females about their future devotion and favor females that are good
at spotting deception; and the better one side gets, the better the other
side gets. It's a vicious spiral of treachery and wariness—even if, in
a sufficiently subtle species, it may assume the form of soft kisses,
murmured endearments, and ingenuous demurrals.

At least it's a vicious spiral *in theory*. Moving beyond all this
theoretical speculation and into the realm of concrete evidence—
actually glimpsing the seamy underside of kisses and endearments—

is tricky. Evolutionary psychologists have made only meager progress. True, one study found that males, markedly more than females, report depicting themselves as more kind, sincere, and trustworthy than they actually are.[12] But that sort of false advertising may be only half the story, and the other half is much harder to get at. As Trivers didn't note in his 1972 paper, but did note four years later, one effective way to deceive someone is to believe what you're saying. In this context, that means being blinded by love—to feel deep affection for a woman who, after a few months of sex, may grow markedly less adorable.[13] This, indeed, is the great moral escape hatch for men who persist in a pattern of elaborate seduction and crisp, if anguished, abandonment. "I loved her at the time," they can movingly recall, if pressed on the matter.

This isn't to say that a man's affections are chronically delusional, that every swoon is tactical self-deception. Sometimes men *do* make good on their vows of eternal devotion. Besides, in one sense, an out-and-out lie is impossible. There's no way of knowing in mid-swoon, either at the conscious or unconscious level, what the future holds. Maybe some more genetically auspicious mate will show up three years from now; then again, maybe the man will suffer some grave misfortune that renders him unmarketable, turning his spouse into his only reproductive hope. But, in the face of uncertainty as to how much commitment lies ahead, natural selection would likely err on the side of exaggeration, so long as it makes sex more likely and doesn't bring counterbalancing costs.

There probably would have been *some* such costs in the intimate social environment of our evolution. Leaving town, or at least village, wasn't a simple matter back then, so blatantly false promises might quickly catch up with a man—in the form of lowered credibility or even shortened life span; the anthropological archives contain stories about men who take vengeance on behalf of a betrayed sister or daughter.[14]

Also, the supply of potentially betrayable women wasn't nearly what it is in the modern world. As Donald Symons has noted, in the average hunter-gatherer society, every man who can snare a wife does, and virtually every woman is married by the time she's fertile. There probably was no thriving singles scene in the ancestral environment, except one involving adolescent girls during the fruitless phase between first menstruation and fertility. Symons believes that the lifestyle of the modern philandering bachelor—seducing and abandoning available women year after year after year, without making any of them targets for ongoing investment—is not a distinct, evolved sexual strategy. It is just what happens when you take the male mind, with its preference for varied sex partners, and put it in a big city replete with contraceptive technology.

Still, even if the ancestral environment wasn't full of single women sitting alone after one-night stands muttering "Men are scum," there were reasons to guard against males who exaggerate commitment. Divorce can happen in hunter-gatherer societies; men do up and leave after fathering a child or two, and may even move to another village. And polygamy is often an option. A man may vow that his bride will stay at the center of his life, and then, once married, spend half his time trying to woo another wife—or, worse still, succeed, and divert resources away from his first wife's children. Given such prospects, a woman's genes would be well served by her early and careful scrutiny of a man's likely devotion. In any event, the gauging of a man's commitment does seem to be part of human female psychology; and male psychology does seem inclined to sometimes encourage a false reading.

That male commitment is in limited supply—that each man has only so much time and energy to invest in offspring—is one reason females in our species defy stereotypes prevalent elsewhere in the animal kingdom. Females in *low*-MPI species—that is, in most sexual species—have no great rivalry with one another. Even if dozens of them have their hearts set on a single, genetically optimal male, he can, and gladly will, fulfill their dreams; copulation doesn't take long. But in a high-MPI species such as ours, where a female's ideal is to *monopolize* her dream mate—steer his social and material resources toward her offspring—competition with other females is inevitable. In other words: high male parental investment makes sexual selection work in two directions at once. Not only have males evolved to compete for scarce female eggs; females have evolved to compete for scarce male investment.

Sexual selection, to be sure, seems to have been more intense among men than among women. And it has favored different sorts of traits in the two. After all, the things women do to gain investment from men are different from the things men do to gain sexual access to women. (Women aren't—to take the most obvious example— designed for physical combat with each other, as men are.) The point is simply that, whatever each sex must do to get what it wants from the other, both sexes should be inclined to do it with zest. Females in a high-MPI species will hardly be passive and guileless. And they will sometimes be the natural enemies of one another.

WHAT DO MEN WANT?

It would be misleading to say that males in a high-male-parental-investment species are selective about mates, but in theory they are at least *selectively* selective. They will, on the one hand, have sex with just about anything that moves, given an easy chance, like males in a low-MPI species. On the other hand, when it comes to finding a female for a long-term joint venture, discretion makes sense; males can undertake only so many ventures over a lifetime, so the genes that the partner brings to the project—genes for robustness, brains, whatever—are worth scrutinizing.

The distinction was nicely drawn by a study in which both men and women were asked about the minimal level of intelligence they would accept in a person they were "dating." The average response, for both male and female, was: average intelligence. They were also asked how smart a person would have to be before they would con- sent to sexual relations. The women said: Oh, in that case, markedly *above* average. The men said: Oh, in that case, markedly *below* average. [15]

Otherwise, the responses of male and female moved in lockstep. A partner they were "steadily dating" would have to be much smarter than average, and a marriageable partner would have to be smarter still. This finding, published in 1990, confirmed a prediction Trivers had made in his 1972 paper on parental investment. In a high-MPI species, he wrote, "a male would be selected to differentiate between a female he will only impregnate and a female with whom he will also raise young. Toward the former he should be more eager for sex and less discriminating in choice of sex partner than the female toward him, but toward the latter he should be about as discriminating as she toward him."[16]

As Trivers knew, the nature of the discrimination, if not its intensity, should still differ between male and female. Though both seek general genetic quality, tastes may in other ways diverge. Just as women have special reason to focus on a man's ability to provide resources, men have special reason to focus on the ability to produce babies. That means, among other things, caring greatly about the age of a potential mate, since fertility declines until menopause, when it falls off abruptly. The last thing evolutionary psychologists would expect to find is that a plainly postmenopausal woman is sexually attractive to the average man. They don't find it. (According to Bronislaw Malinowski, Trobriand Islanders considered sex with an old woman "indecorous, ludicrous, and unaesthetic.")[17] Even before menopause, age matters, especially in a long-term mate; the younger a woman, the more children she can bear. In every one of Buss's thirty-seven cultures, males preferred younger mates (and females preferred older mates).

The importance of youth in a female mate may help explain the extreme male concern with physical attractiveness in a spouse (a concern that Buss also documented in all thirty-seven cultures). The generic "beautiful woman"—yes, she has actually been assembled, in a study that collated the seemingly diverse tastes of different men—has large eyes and a small nose. Since her eyes will look smaller and her nose larger as she ages, these components of "beauty" are also marks of youth, and thus of fertility.[18] Women can afford to be more open-minded about looks; an oldish man, unlike an oldish woman, is probably fertile.

Another reason for the relative flexibility of females on the question of facial attractiveness may be that a woman has other things to (consciously or unconsciously) worry about. Such as: Will he provide for the kids? When people see a beautiful woman with an ugly man, they typically assume he has lots of money or status. Researchers have actually gone to the trouble of showing that people make this inference, and that the inference is often correct.[19]

When it comes to assessing character—to figuring out if you can *trust* a mate—a male's discernment may again differ from a female's, because the kind of treachery that threatens his genes is different from the kind that threatens hers. Whereas the woman's natural fear is the withdrawal of his investment, his natural fear is that the investment is misplaced. Not long for this world are the genes of a man who spends his time rearing children who aren't his. Trivers noted in 1972 that, in a species with high male parental investment and internal fertilization, "adaptations should evolve to help guarantee that the female's offspring are also his own."[20]

All of this may sound highly theoretical—and of course it is. But this theory, unlike the theory about male love sometimes being finely crafted self-delusion, is readily tested. Years after Trivers suggested that anticuckoldry technology might be built into men, Martin Daly and Margo Wilson found some. They realized that if indeed a man's great Darwinian peril is cuckoldry, and a woman's is desertion, then male and female jealousy should differ.[21] Male jealousy should focus on *sexual* infidelity, and males should be quite unforgiving of it; a female, though she'll hardly applaud a partner's extracurricular activities, since they consume time and divert resources, should be more concerned with *emotional* infidelity—the sort of magnetic commitment to another woman that could eventually lead to a much larger diversion of resources.

These predictions have been confirmed—by eons of folk wisdom and, over the past few decades, by considerable data. What drives men craziest is the thought of their mate in bed with another man; they don't dwell as much as women do on any attendant emotional attachment, or the possible loss of the mate's time and attention. Wives, for their part, do find the sheerly sexual infidelity of husbands traumatic, and do respond harshly to it, but the long-run effect is often a self-improvement campaign: lose weight, wear makeup, "win him back." Husbands tend to respond to infidelity with rage; and even after it subsides, they often have trouble contemplating a continued relationship with the infidel.[22]

Looking back, Daly and Wilson saw that this basic pattern had been recorded (though not stressed) by psychologists before the theory of parental investment came along to explain it. But evolutionary psychologists have now confirmed the pattern in new and excruciating detail. David Buss placed electrodes on men and women and had them envision their mates doing various disturbing things. When men imagined sexual infidelity, their heart rates took leaps of a magnitude typically induced by three successive cups of coffee. They sweated. Their brows wrinkled. When they imagined instead a budding emotional attachment, they calmed down, though not quite to their normal level. For women, things were reversed: envisioning *emotional* infidelity—redirected love, not supplementary sex—brought the deeper physiological distress.[23]

The logic behind male jealousy isn't what it used to be. These days some adulterous women use contraception and thus don't, in fact, dupe their husbands into spending two decades shepherding another man's genes. But the weakening of the logic doesn't seem to have weakened the jealousy. For the average husband, the fact that his wife inserted a diaphragm before copulating with her tennis instructor will not be a major source of consolation.

The classic example of an adaptation that has outlived its logic is the sweet tooth. Our fondness for sweetness was designed for an environment in which fruit existed but candy didn't. Now that a sweet tooth can bring obesity, people try to control their cravings, and sometimes they succeed. But their methods are usually roundabout, and few people find them easy; the basic sense that sweetness feels good is almost unalterable (except by, say, repeatedly pairing a sweet taste with a painful shock). Similarly, the basic impulse toward jealousy is very hard to erase. Still, people can muster some control over the impulse, and, moreover, can muster much control over some forms of its expression, such as violence, given a sufficiently powerful reason. Prison, for example.

WHAT ELSE DO WOMEN WANT?

Before further exploring the grave imprint that cuckoldry has left on the male psyche, we might ask why it would exist. Why would a woman cheat on a man, if that won't increase the number of her progeny—and if, moreover, she thus risks incurring the wrath, and losing the investment, of her mate? What reward could justify such a gamble? There are more possible answers to this question than you might imagine.

First, there is what biologists call "resource extraction." If female humans, like female hanging flies, can get gifts in exchange for sex, then the more sex partners, the more gifts. Our closest primate relatives act out this logic. Female bonobos are often willing to provide sex in exchange for a hunk of meat. Among common chimpanzees, the food-for-sex swap is less explicit but is evident; male chimps are more likely to give meat to a female when she exhibits the red vaginal swelling that signifies ovulation.[24]

Human females, of course, *don't* advertise their ovulation. One theory about this "cryptic ovulation" sees it as an adaptation designed to expand the period during which they can extract resources. Men may lavish gifts on them well before or past ovulation and receive sex in return, blissfully oblivious to the fruitlessness of their conquest. Nisa, a woman in a !Kung San hunter-gatherer village, spoke candidly with an anthropologist about the material rewards of multiple sex partners. "One man can give you very little. One man gives you only one kind of food to eat. But when you have lovers, one brings you something and another brings you something else. One comes at night with meat, another with money, another with beads. Your husband also does things and gives them to you."[25]

Another reason women might copulate with more than one man—and another advantage of concealed ovulation—is to leave several men under the impression that they *might* be the father of particular offspring. Across primate species, there is a rough correlation between a male's kindness to youngsters and the chances that he is their father. The dominant male gorilla, with his celestial sexual stature, can rest pretty much assured that the youngsters in his troop are his; and, although not demonstrative by comparison with a human father, he is indulgent of them and reliably protective. At the other end of the spectrum, male langur monkeys kill infants sired by others as a kind of sexual icebreaker, a prelude to pairing up with the (former) mother.[26] What better way to return her to ovulation—by putting an emphatic end to her breast-feeding—and to focus her energies on the offspring to come?

Anyone tempted to launch into a sweeping indictment of langur morality should first note that infanticide on grounds of infidelity has been acceptable in various human societies. In two societies men have been known to demand, upon marrying women with a past, that their babies be killed.[27] And among the Ache hunter-gatherers of Paraguay, men sometimes collectively decide to kill a newly fatherless child. Even leaving murder aside, life can be hard on children without a devoted father. Ache children raised by stepfathers after their biological fathers die are half as likely to live to age fifteen as children whose parents stay alive and together.[28] For a woman in the ancestral environment, then, the benefits of multiple sex partners could have ranged from their not killing her youngster to their defending or otherwise aiding her youngster.

This logic doesn't depend on the sex partners' consciously mulling it over. Male gorillas and langurs, like the Trobriand Islanders as depicted by Malinowski, are not conscious of biological paternity. Still, the behavior of males in all three cases reflects an implicit recognition. Genes making males unconsciously sensitive to cues that certain youngsters may or may not be carrying their genes have flourished. A gene that says, or at least whispers, "Be nice to children if you've had a fair amount of sex with their mothers" will do better than a gene that says, "Steal food from children even if you were having regular sex with their mothers months before birth."

This "seeds of confusion" theory of female promiscuity has been championed by the anthropologist Sarah Blaffer Hrdy. Hrdy has described herself as a feminist sociobiologist, and she may take a more than scientific interest in arguing that female primates tend to be "highly competitive . . . sexually assertive individuals."[29] Then again, male Darwinians may get a certain thrill from saying males are built for lifelong sex-a-thons. Scientific theories spring from many sources. The only question in the end is whether they work.

Both of these theories of female promiscuity—"resource extraction" and "seeds of confusion"—could in principle apply to a mateless woman as well as a married one. Indeed, both would make sense for a species with little or no male parental investment, and thus may help explain the extreme promiscuity of female chimpanzees and bonobos. But there is a third theory that grows uniquely out of the dynamics of male parental investment, and thus has special application to wives: the "best of both worlds" theory.

In a high-MPI species, the female seeks two things: good genes and high ongoing investment. She may not find them in the same package. One solution would be to trick a devoted but not especially brawny or brainy mate into raising the offspring of another male. Again, cryptic ovulation would come in handy, as a treachery facilitator. It's fairly easy for a man to keep rivals from impregnating his mate if her brief phase of fertility is plainly visible; but if she appears equally fertile all month, surveillance becomes a problem. This is exactly the confusion a female would want to create if her goal is to draw investment from one man and genes from another.[30] Of course, the female may not consciously "want" this "goal." And she may not be consciously aware of when she's ovulating. But at some level she may be keeping track.

Theories involving so much subconscious subterfuge may sound too clever by half, especially to people not steeped in the cynical logic of natural selection. But there is some evidence that women are more sexually active around ovulation.[31] And two studies have found that women going to a singles bar wear more jewelry and makeup when near ovulation.[32] These adornments, it seems, have the advertising value of a chimpanzee's pink genital swelling, attracting a number of men for the woman to choose from. And these decked-out women did indeed tend to have more physical contact with men in the course of the evening.

Another study, by the British biologists R. Robin Baker and Mark Bellis, found that women who cheat on their mates are more likely to do so around ovulation. This suggests that often the secret lover's genes, not just his resources, are indeed what they're after.[33]

Whatever the reason(s) women cheat on their mates (or, as biologists value-neutrally put it, have "extra-pair copulations"), there's no denying that they do. Blood tests show that in some urban areas more than one fourth of the children may be sired by someone other than the father of record. And even in a !Kung San village, which, like the ancestral environment, is so intimate as to make covert liaison tricky, one in fifty children was found to have misassigned paternity.[34] Female infidelity appears to have a long history.

Indeed, if female infidelity *weren't* a long-standing part of life in this species, why would distinctively maniacal male jealousy have evolved? At the same time, that men so often invest heavily in the children of their mates suggests that cuckoldry hasn't been rampant;

if it had, genes encouraging this investment would long ago have run into a dead end.[35] The minds of men are an evolutionary record of the past behavior of women. And vice versa.

If a "psychological" record seems too vague, consider a more plainly physiological bit of data: human testicles—or, more exactly, the ratio of average testes weight to average male body weight. Chimpanzees and other species with high relative testes weights have "multimale breeding systems," in which females are quite promiscuous.[36] Species with low relative testes weights are either monogamous (gibbons, for example) or polygynous (gorillas), with one male monopolizing several families. (*Polygamous* is the more general term, denoting a male *or* a female that has more than one mate.) The explanation is simple. When females commonly breed with many different males, male genes can profit by producing lots of semen for their transportation. Which male gets his DNA into a given egg may be a question of sheer volume, as competing hordes of sperm do subterranean battle. A species' testicles are thus a record of its females' sexual adventure over the ages. In our species, relative testes weight falls between that of the chimpanzee and the gorilla, suggesting that women, while not nearly as wild as chimpanzee females, are, by nature, somewhat adventurous.

Of course, adventurous doesn't mean unfaithful. Maybe women in the ancestral environment had their wild, unattached periods—during which fairly weighty testicles paid off for men—as well as their devoted, monogamous periods. Then again, maybe not. Consider a truer record of female infidelity: variable sperm density. You might think that the number of sperm cells in a husband's ejaculate would depend only on how long it's been since he last had sex. Wrong. According to work by Baker and Bellis, the quantity of sperm depends heavily on the amount of time a man's mate has been out of his sight lately.[37] The more chances a woman has had to collect sperm from other males, the more profusely her mate sends in his own troops. Again: that natural selection designed such a clever weapon is evidence of something for the weapon to combat.

It is also evidence that natural selection is fully capable of designing equally clever psychological weapons, ranging from furious jealousy to the seemingly paradoxical tendency of some men to be sexually aroused by the thought of their mate in bed with another man. Or, more generally: the tendency of men to view women as possessions. In a 1992 paper called "The Man Who Mistook His Wife for a Chattel," Wilson and Daly wrote that "men lay claim to particular women as songbirds lay claim to territories, as lions lay claim to a kill, or as people of both sexes lay claim to valuables. . . . [R]eferring to man's view of woman as 'proprietary' is more than a metaphor: Some of the same mental algorithms are apparently activated in the marital and mercantile spheres."[38]

The theoretical upshot of all this is another evolutionary arms race. As men grow more attuned to the threat of cuckoldry, women should get better at convincing a man that their adoration borders on awe, their fidelity on the saintly. And they may partly convince themselves too, just for good measure. Indeed, given the calamitous fallout from infidelity uncovered—likely desertion by the offended male, and possible violence—female self-deception may be finely honed. It could be adaptive for a married woman to not *feel* chronically concerned with sex, even if her unconscious mind is keeping track of prospects and will notify her when ardor is warranted.

THE MADONNA-WHORE DICHOTOMY

Anticuckoldry technology could come in handy not just when a man has a mate, but earlier, in choosing her. If available females differ in their promiscuity, and if the more promiscuous ones tend to make less faithful wives, natural selection might incline men to discriminate accordingly. Promiscuous women would be welcome as short-term sex partners—indeed, preferable, in some ways, since they can be had with less effort. But they would make poor wife material, a dubious conduit for male parental investment.

What emotional mechanisms—what complex of attractions and aversions—would natural selection use to get males to uncomprehendingly follow this logic? As Donald Symons has noted, one candidate is the famed Madonna-whore dichotomy, the tendency of men to think in terms of "two kinds of women"—the kind they respect and the kind they just sleep with.[39]

One can imagine courtship as, among other things, a process of placing a woman in one category or the other. The test would run roughly as follows. If you find a woman who appears genetically suitable for investment, start spending lots of time with her. If she seems quite taken by you, and yet remains sexually aloof, stick with her. If, on the other hand, she seems eager for sex right away, then by all means oblige her. But if the sex does come that easily, you might want to shift from investment mode into exploitation mode. Her eagerness could mean she'll always be an easy seduction—not a desirable quality in a wife.

Of course, in the case of any particular woman, sexual eagerness may *not* mean she'll always be an easy seduction; maybe she just finds this one man irresistible. But if there is any general correlation between the speed with which a woman succumbs to a man and her likelihood of later cheating on him, then that speed is a statistically valid cue to a matter of great genetic consequence. Faced with the complexity and frequent unpredictability of human behavior, natural selection plays the odds.

Just to add a trifle more ruthlessness to this strategy: the male may actually *encourage* the early sex for which he will ultimately punish the woman. What better way to check for the sort of self-restraint that is so precious in a woman whose children you may invest in? And, if self-restraint proves lacking, what faster way to get the wild oats sown before moving on to worthier terrain?

In its extreme, pathological form—the Madonna-whore *complex*—this dichotomization of women leaves a man unable to have sex with his wife, so holy does she seem. Obviously, this degree of worship isn't likely to have been favored by natural selection. But the more common, more moderate version of the Madonna-whore distinction has the earmarks of an efficient adaptation. It leads men to shower worshipful devotion on the sexually reserved women they want to invest in—exactly the sort of devotion these women will demand before allowing sex. And it lets men guiltlessly exploit the women they don't want to invest in, by consigning them to a category that merits contempt. This general category—the category of reduced, sometimes almost subhuman, moral status—is, as we'll see, a favorite tool of natural selection's; it is put to especially effective use during wars.

In polite company, men sometimes deny that they think differently of a woman who has slept with them casually. And wisely so. To admit that they do would sound morally reactionary. (Even to admit as much to themselves might make it hard to earnestly assure such a woman that they'll still respect her in the morning—sometimes a vital part of foreplay.)

As many modern wives can attest, sleeping with a man early in courtship doesn't doom the prospect of long-term commitment. A man's (largely unconscious) assessment of a woman's likely fidelity presumably involves many things—her reputation, how she looks at other men, how honest she seems generally. And anyway, even in theory the male mind shouldn't be designed to make virginity a prerequisite for investment. The chances of finding a virgin wife vary from man to man and from culture to culture—and to judge by some hunter-gatherer societies, they would have been quite low in the ancestral environment. Presumably males are designed to do the best they can under the circumstances. Though in prudish Victorian England some men may have insisted on virgin wives, the term *Madonna-whore dichotomy* is actually a misnomer for what is surely a more flexible mental tendency.[40]

Still, the flexibility is bounded. There is some level of female promiscuity above which male parental investment plainly makes no genetic sense. If a woman seems to have an unbreakable habit of sleeping with a different man each week, the fact that all women in that culture do the same thing doesn't make her any more logical a spouse. In such a society, men should in theory give up entirely on concentrated parental investment and focus solely on trying to mate with as many women as possible. That is, they should act like chimpanzees.

VICTORIAN SAMOANS

The Madonna-whore dichotomy has long been dismissed as an aberration, another pathological product of Western culture. In particular, the Victorians, with their extraordinary emphasis on virginity and their professed disdain for illicit sex, are held responsible for nourishing, even inventing, the pathology. If only men in Darwin's day had been more relaxed about sex, like the men in non-Western, sexually liberated societies. How different things would be now!

The trouble is, those idyllic, non-Western societies seem to have existed only in the minds of a few misguided, if influential, academics. The classic example is Margaret Mead, one of several prominent anthropologists who early this century reacted to the political misuses of Darwinism by stressing the malleability of the human species and asserting the near absence of human nature. Mead's best-known book, *Coming of Age in Samoa,* created a sensation upon its appearance in 1928. She seemed to have found a culture nearly devoid of many Western evils: status hierarchies, intense competition, and all kinds of needless anxieties about sex. Here in Samoa, Mead wrote, girls postpone marriage "through as many years of casual love-making as possible." Romantic love "as it occurs in our civilisation," bound up with ideas of "exclusiveness, jealousy and undeviating fidelity," simply "does not occur in Samoa."[41] What a wonderful place!

It is hard to exaggerate the influence of Mead's findings on twentieth-century thought. Claims about human nature are always precarious, vulnerable to the discovery of even a single culture in which its elements are fundamentally lacking. For much of this century, such claims have been ritually met with a single question: "What about Samoa?"

In 1983 the anthropologist Derek Freeman published a book called *Margaret Mead and Samoa: The Making and Unmaking of an Anthropological Myth.* Freeman had spent nearly six years in Samoa (Mead had spent nine months, and hadn't spoken the language when she arrived), and was well versed in accounts of its earlier history, before Western contact had much changed it. His book left Mead's reputation as a great anthropologist in serious disarray. He depicted her as a naïf, a twenty-three-year-old idealist who went to Samoa steeped in fashionable cultural determinism, chose not to live among the natives, and then, dependent for her data on scheduled interviews, was duped by Samoan girls who made a game of misleading her. Freeman assaulted Mead's data broadly—the supposed dearth of status competition, the simple bliss of Samoan adolescence—but for present purposes what matters is the sex: the purportedly minor significance of jealousy and male possessiveness, the seeming indifference of men to the Madonna-whore dichotomy.

Actually, on close examination, Mead's point-by-point findings turn out to be less radical than her glossy, well-publicized generalizations. She conceded that Samoan males took a certain pride in the conquest of a virgin. She also noted that each tribe had a ceremonial virgin—a girl of good breeding, often a chief's daughter, who was carefully guarded until, upon marriage, she was manually deflowered, with the blood from her hymen proving her purity. But this girl, Mead insisted, was an aberration, "excepted" from the "free and easy experimentation" that was the norm. Parents of lower rank "complacently ignore" their daughters' sexual experimentation.[42] Mead granted, almost under her breath, that a virginity test was "theoretically" performed "at weddings of people of all ranks," but she dismissed the ceremony as easily and often evaded.

Freeman raised the volume of Mead's more hushed observations and pointed out some things she had failed entirely to note. The value of virgins was so great in the eyes of marriageable men, he wrote, that an adolescent female of any social rank was monitored by her brothers, who would "upbraid, and sometimes beat" her if they found her with "a boy suspected of having designs on her virginity." As for the suspected boy, he was "liable to be assaulted with great ferocity." Young men who fared poorly in the mating game sometimes secured a mate by sneaking in at night, forcibly deflowering a woman, and then threatening to disclose her corruption unless she agreed to marriage (perhaps in the form of elopement, the surest way to avoid a virginity test). A woman found on her wedding day not to be a virgin was publicly denounced with a term meaning, roughly, "whore." In Samoan lore, one deflowered woman is described as a "wanton woman, like an empty shell exposed by the ebbing tide!" A song performed at defloration ceremonies went like this: "All others have failed to achieve entry, all others have failed to achieve entry. . . . He is first by being foremost, being first he is foremost; O to be foremost!"[43] These are not the hallmarks of a sexually liberated culture.

It now appears that some of the supposed Western aberrations that Mead found lacking in Samoa had if anything been *suppressed* by Western influence. Missionaries, Freeman noted, had made virginity testing less public—performed in a house, behind a screen. In "former days," as Mead herself wrote, if the tribe's ceremonial virgin was found at her wedding to be less than virginal, "her female relatives fell upon and beat her with stones, disfiguring and sometimes fatally injuring the girl who had shamed their house."[44]

So too with the Samoan jealousy that, Mead stressed, was so muted by Western standards: Westerners may have done the muting. Mead noted that a husband who caught his wife in adultery might be appeased by a harmless ritual that, as she depicted it, would end in an air of bonhomie. The male offender would bring men of his family, sit outside the victimized husband's house in supplication, offering finery in recompense, until forgiveness was forthcoming and everyone buried the hatchet over dinner. Of course, "in olden days," Mead observed, the offended man might "take a club and together with his relatives go out and kill those who sit without."[45]

That violence became less frequent under Christian influence is, of course, a testament to human malleability. But if we are ever to fathom the complex parameters of that malleability, we must be clear about which is the core disposition and which is the modifying influence. Time and again, Mead, along with her whole cohort of mid-twentieth-century cultural determinists, got things backwards.

Darwinism helps set the record straight. A new generation of Darwinian anthropologists is combing old ethnographies and conducting new field studies, finding things past anthropologists didn't stress, or even notice. Many candidates for "human nature" are emerging. And one of the more viable is the Madonna-whore dichotomy. In exotic cultures from Samoa to Mangaia to the land of the Ache in South America, a reputation for extreme promiscuity is something men actively avoid in a long-term mate.[46] And an analysis of folklore reveals the "good girl/bad girl" polarity to be a chronically recurring image—in the Far East, in Islamic states, in Europe, even in pre-Columbian America.[47]

Meanwhile, in the psychology laboratory, David Buss has found evidence that men do dichotomize between short-term and long-term mates. Cues suggesting promiscuity (a low-cut dress, perhaps, or aggressive body language) make a woman more attractive as a short-term mate and less attractive as a long-term mate. Cues suggesting a lack of sexual experience work the other way around.[48]

For now, the hypothesis that the Madonna-whore dichotomy has at least some inherent basis rests on strong theoretical expectation and considerable, though hardly exhaustive, anthropological and psychological evidence. There is also, of course, the testimony of experienced mothers from many eras who have warned their daughters what will happen if a man gets the impression that they're "that kind of girl": he won't "respect" them anymore.

FAST AND SLOW WOMEN

The Madonna-whore distinction is a dichotomy imposed on a continuum. In real life, women aren't either "fast" or "slow"; they are promiscuous to various degrees, ranging from not at all to quite. So the question of why some women are of one type and others of the other has no meaning. But there is meaning in the question of why women are nearer one end of the spectrum than the other— why women differ in their general degree of sexual reserve. And for that matter, what about men? Why do some men seem capable of unswerving monogamy, and others so inclined to depart from that ideal to various degrees? Is this difference—between Madonnas and whores, between dads and cads—in the genes? The answer is a definite yes. But the only reason the answer is definite is that the phrase "in the genes" is so ambiguous as to be essentially meaningless.

Let's start with the popular conception of "in the genes." Are some women, from the moment their father's sperm meets their mother's egg, all but destined to be Madonnas, while others are almost certain to be whores? Are some men equally bound to be cads, and others dads?

For both men and women, the answer is: unlikely, but not impossible. As a rule, two extremely different alternative traits will not both be preserved by natural selection. One or the other is usually at least slightly more conducive to genetic proliferation. However marginal its edge, it should win out, given enough time.[49] That's why almost all of the genes in you are also in the average inhabitant of any land in the world. But there is something called "frequency-dependent" selection, in which the value of a trait declines as it becomes more common, so that natural selection places a ceiling on its predominance, thus leaving room for the alternative.

Consider the bluegill sunfish.[50] The average bluegill male grows up, builds a bunch of nests, waits for females to lay eggs, then fertilizes the eggs and guards them. He is an upstanding member of the community. But he may have as many as 150 nests to tend, a fact that leaves him vulnerable to a second, less responsible kind of male, a drifter. The drifter sneaks around, surreptitiously fertilizes eggs, and then darts off, leaving them to be tended by their duped custodian. At a certain stage in life, drifters even don the color and behavior of females to mask their covert operations.

You can see how the balance between drifters and their victims is maintained. The drifters must do fairly well in reproductive terms; otherwise they wouldn't be around. But as this success makes their fraction of the population grow, the success itself diminishes, because the relative supply of upstanding, exploitable males—the drifters' meal ticket—shrinks. This is a situation in which success is its own punishment. The more drifters there are, the fewer offspring per drifter there are.

In theory, the drifter fraction of the population should grow until the average drifter is having as many offspring as the average upstanding bluegill. At that point, any shift in the fraction—growth or shrinkage—will change the value of the two strategies in a way that tends to reverse the shift. This equilibrium is known as an "evolutionarily stable" state, a term coined by the British biologist John Maynard Smith, who, during the 1970s, fully developed the idea of frequency-dependent selection.[51] Bluegill drifters, presumably, long ago reached their evolutionarily stable fraction of the population, which seems to be about one fifth.

The dynamics of sexual treachery are different for humans than for bluegill sunfish, in part because of the mammalian penchant for internal fertilization. But Richard Dawkins has shown, with an abstract analysis applicable to our species, that Maynard Smith's logic can, in principle, fit us too. In other words: one can imagine a situation in which neither coy nor fast women, and neither cads nor dads, have a monopoly on the ideal strategy. Rather, the success of each strategy varies with the prevalence of the three other strategies, and the population tends toward equilibrium. For example, with one set of assumptions, Dawkins found that five-sixths of the females would be coy, and five-eighths of the males would be faithful.[52]

Now, having comprehended this fact, you are advised to forget it. Don't just forget the fractions themselves, which, obviously, grow out of arbitrary assumptions within a highly artificial model. Forget the whole idea that each individual would be firmly bound to one strategy or the other.

As Maynard Smith and Dawkins have noted, evolution equilibrates to an equally stable state if you assume that the magic proportions are found *within* individuals—that is, if each female is coy on five-sixths of her mating opportunities, and each male is coy on five-eighths of his. And that's true even if the fractions are *randomly* realized—if each person just rolls dice on each encounter to decide what to do. Imagine how much more effective it is for the person to ponder each situation (consciously or unconsciously) and make an informed guess as to which strategy is more propitious under the circumstances.

Or imagine a different kind of flexibility: a developmental program that, during childhood, assesses the local social environment and then, by adulthood, inclines the person toward the strategy more likely to pay off. To put this in bluegill terms: imagine a male that during its early years checks out the local environment, calculates the prevalence of exploitable, upstanding males, and *then* decides—or, at least, "decides"—whether to become a drifter. This plasticity should eventually dominate the population, pushing the two more rigid strategies into oblivion.

The moral of the story is that limberness, given the opportunity, usually wins out over stiffness. In fact, limberness seems to have won a partial victory even in the bluegill sunfish, which isn't exactly known for its highly developed cerebral cortex. Though some genes incline a male bluegill to one strategy, and others to the other, the inclination isn't complete; the male absorbs local data before "deciding" which strategy to adopt.[53] Obviously, when you move from fish to us, the likely extent of flexibility grows. We have huge brains whose whole reason for being is deft adjustment to variable conditions. Given the many things about a person's social environment that can alter the value of being a Madonna versus a whore, a cad versus a dad—including the way other people react to the person's particular assets and liabilities—natural selection would be uncharacteristically obtuse not to favor genes that build brains sensitive to these things.

So too in many other realms. The value of being a given "type" of person—cooperative, say, or stingy—has depended, during evolution, on things that vary from time to time, place to place, person to person. Genes that irrevocably committed our ancestors to one personality type should in theory have lost out to genes that let the personality solidify gracefully.

This is not a matter of consensus. There are in the literature a few articles with titles like "The Evolution of the 'Con Artist.'"[54] And, to return to the realm of Madonnas and whores, there is a theory that some women are innately inclined to pursue a "sexy son" strategy: they mate promiscuously with sexually attractive men (handsome, brainy, brawny, and so on), risking the high male parental investment they might extract if more Madonnaish but gaining the likelihood that any sons will be, like their fathers, attractive and therefore prolific. Such theories are interesting, but they all face the same obstacle: with con artists as with promiscuous women, however effective the strategy, it is even more effective when flexible—when it can be abandoned amid signs of likely failure.[55] And the human brain is a pretty flexible thing.

To stress this flexibility isn't to say that all people are born psychologically identical, that all differences in personality emerge from environment. There plainly are important genetic differences for such traits as nervousness and extroversion. The "heritability" of these traits is around .4; that is, about 40 percent of individual differences in these traits can be explained by genetic differences. (By comparison, the heritability of height is around .9; about 10 percent of the difference in height among individuals is due to nutritional and other environmental differences.) The question is *why* the undoubtedly important genetic variation in personality exists. Do different degrees of genetic disposition toward extroversion represent different personality "types," each of which has stabilized after a very elaborate process of frequency-dependent selection? (Though frequency dependence is classically analyzed in terms of two or three distinct strategies, it could also yield a more finely graded array.) Or are the differing genetic dispositions just "noise"—some incidental by-product of evolution, not specifically favored by natural selection? No one knows, and evolutionary psychologists differ in their suspicions.[56] What they agree on is that a big part of the story of personality differences is the evolution of malleability, what they call "developmental plasticity."

This emphasis on psychological development doesn't leave us back where social scientists were twenty-five years ago, attributing everything they saw to often unspecified "environmental forces." A primary—perhaps *the* primary—promise of evolutionary psychology is to help specify the forces, to generate good theories of personality development. In other words: evolutionary psychology can help us see not only the "knobs" of human nature, but also how the knobs are tuned. It not only shows us that (and why) men in all cultures are quite attracted to sexual variety, but can suggest what circumstances make some men more obsessed with it than others; it not only shows us that (and why) women in all cultures are more sexually reserved, but promises to help us figure out how some women come to defy this stereotype.

A good example lies in Robert Trivers's 1972 paper on parental investment. Trivers noted two patterns that social scientists had already uncovered: (1) the more attractive an adolescent girl, the more likely she is to "marry up"—marry a man of higher socioeconomic status; and (2) the more sexually active an adolescent girl, the less likely she is to marry up.

To begin with, these two patterns make Darwinian sense independently. A wealthy, high-status male often has a broad range of aspiring wives to choose from. So he tends to choose a good-looking woman who is also relatively Madonnaish. Trivers took the analysis further. Is it possible, he asked, "that females adjust their reproductive strategies in adolescence to their own assets"?[57] In other words, maybe adolescent girls who get early social feedback affirming their beauty make the most of it, becoming sexually reserved and thus encouraging long-term investment by high-status males who are looking for pretty Madonnas. Less attractive women, with less chance to hit the jackpot via sexual reserve, become more promiscuous, extracting small chunks of resources from a series of males. Though this promiscuity may somewhat lower their values as wives, it wouldn't, in the ancestral environment, have doomed their chances of finding a husband. In the average hunter-gatherer society, almost any fertile woman can find a husband, even if he's far from ideal, or she has to share him with another woman.

DARWINISM AND PUBLIC POLICY

The Trivers scenario doesn't imply a *conscious* decision by attractive women to guard their jewels (though that may play a role, and, what's more, parents may be genetically inclined to encourage a daughter's sexual reserve with special force when she is pretty). By the same token, we aren't necessarily talking about unattractive women who "realize" they can't be choosy and start having sex on less than ideal Darwinian terms. The mechanism at work might well be subconscious, a gradual molding of sexual strategy—read: "moral values"—by adolescent experience.

Theories like this one matter. There has been much talk about the problem of unwed motherhood among teenagers, especially poor teenagers. But no one really knows how sexual habits get shaped, or how firmly fixed they then are. There is much talk about boosting "self-esteem," but little understanding of what self-esteem is, what it's for, or what it does.

Evolutionary psychology can't yet confidently provide the missing basis for these discussions. But the problem isn't a shortage of plausible theories; it's a shortage of studies to test the theories. The Trivers theory has sat in limbo for two decades. In 1992, one psychologist did find what the theory predicts—a correlation between a woman's self-perception and her sexual habits: the less attractive she thinks she is, the more sex partners she has had. But another scholar didn't find the predicted correlation—and, more to the point, *neither* study was conducted specifically to test Trivers's theory, of which both scholars were unaware.[58] For now, this is the state of evolutionary psychology: so much fertile terrain, so few farmers.

Eventually, the main drift of Trivers's theory, if not the theory itself, will likely be vindicated. That is: women's sexual strategies probably depend on the likely (genetic) profitability of each strategy, given prevailing circumstances. But those circumstances go beyond what Trivers stressed—a particular woman's desirability. Another factor is the general availability of male parental investment. This factor surely fluctuated in the ancestral environment. For example, a village that had just invaded a neighboring village might have a suddenly elevated ratio of women to men—not just because of male casualties, but because victorious warriors commonly kill or vanquish enemy men and keep their women.[59] Overnight, a young woman's prospects for receiving a man's undivided investment could thus plummet. Famine, or sudden abundance, might also alter investment patterns. Given these currents of change, any genes that helped women navigate them would, in theory, have flourished.

There is tentative evidence that they did. According to a study by the anthropologist Elizabeth Cashdan, women who perceive men in general as pursuing no-obligation sex are more likely to wear provocative clothes and have sex often than women who see men as generally willing to invest in offspring.[60] Though some of these women may be conscious of the connection between local conditions and their lifestyle, that isn't necessary. Women surrounded by men who are unwilling or unable to serve as devoted fathers may simply feel a deepened attraction to sex without commitment—feel, in other words, a relaxation of "moral" constraint. And perhaps if market conditions suddenly improve—if the male to female ratio rises, or if men for some other reason shift toward a high-investment strategy— women's sexual attractions, and moral sensibilities, shift accordingly.

All of this is necessarily speculative at this early stage in evolutionary psychology's growth. But already we can see the sort of light that will increasingly be shed. For example, "self-esteem" almost certainly isn't the same, either in its sources or in its effects, for boys and girls. For teenage girls, feedback reflecting great beauty may, as Trivers suggested, bring high self-esteem, which in turn encourages sexual restraint. For boys, extremely high self-esteem could well have the opposite effect: it may lead them to seek with particular intensity the short-term sexual conquests that are, in fact, more open to a good-looking, high-status male. In many high schools, a handsome, star athlete is referred to, only half-jokingly, as a "stud." And, for those who insist on scientific verification of the obvious: good-looking men do have more sex partners than the average man.[61] (Women report putting more emphasis on a sex partner's looks when they don't expect the relationship to last; they are apparently willing, unconsciously, to trade off parental investment for good genes.)[62]

Once a high-self-esteem male is married, he may not be notable for his devotion. Presumably his various assets still make philandering a viable lifestyle, even if it's now covert. (And you never know when an outside escapade will take on a life of its own, and lead to desertion.) Men with more moderate self-esteem may make more committed, if otherwise less desirable, husbands. With fewer chances at extramarital dalliance, and perhaps more insecurity about their own mate's fidelity, they may focus their energy and attention toward family. Meanwhile, men with *extremely* low self-esteem, given continued frustration with women, may eventually resort to rape. There is ongoing debate within evolutionary psychology over whether rape is an adaptation, a designed strategy that any boy might grow up to adopt, given sufficiently discouraging feedback from his social environment. Certainly rape surfaces in a wide variety of cultures, and often under the expected circumstances: when men have had trouble finding attractive women by legitimate means. One (non-Darwinian) study found the typical rapist to possess "deep-seated doubts about his adequacy and competency as a person. He lacks a sense of confidence in himself as a man in both sexual and nonsexual areas."[63]

A second sort of light shed by the new Darwinian paradigm may illuminate links between poverty and sexual morality. Women living in an environment where few men have the ability and/or desire to support a family might naturally grow amenable to sex without commitment. (Often in history—including Victorian England—women in the "lower classes" have had a reputation for loose morals.)[64] It is too soon to assert this confidently, or to infer that inner-city sexual mores would change markedly if income levels did. But it is noteworthy, at least, that evolutionary psychology, with its emphasis on the role of environment, may wind up highlighting the social costs of poverty, and thus at times lend strength to liberal policy prescriptions, defying old stereotypes of Darwinism as right-wing.

Of course, one could argue that various policy implications ensue from any given theory. And one can dream up wholly different kinds of Darwinian theories about how sexual strategies get shaped.[65] The one thing one *can't* do, I submit, is argue that evolutionary psychology is irrelevant to the whole discussion. The idea that natural selection, acutely attentive to the most subtle elements of design in the lowliest animals, should build huge, exquisitely pliable brains and not make them highly sensitive to environmental cues regarding sex, status, and various other things known to figure centrally in our reproductive prospects—that idea is literally incredible. If we want to know when and how a person's character begins to assume distinct shape, if we want to know how resistant to change the character will subsequently be, we have to look to Darwin. We don't yet know the answers, but we know where they'll come from, and that knowledge helps us phrase the questions more sharply.

THE FAMILY THAT STAYS TOGETHER

Much of the attention paid to the "short-term" sexual strategies of women—whether unattached women willing to settle for a one-night stand, or attached women sneaking out on a mate—is fairly recent. Sociobiological discussion during the 1970s, at least in its popular form, tended to depict men as wild, libidinous creatures who roamed the landscape looking for women to dupe and exploit; women were often depicted as dupes and exploitees. The shift in focus is due largely to the growing number of female Darwinian social scientists, who have patiently explained to their male colleagues how a woman's psyche looks from the inside.

Even after this restoration of balance, there remains one important sense in which men and women will tend to be, respectively, exploiter

and exploited. As a marriage progresses, the temptation to desert should—in the *average* case—shift toward the man. The reason isn't, as people sometimes assume, that the Darwinian *costs* of marital breakup are greater for the woman. True, if she has a young child and her marriage dissolves, that child may suffer—whether because she can't find a husband willing to commit to a woman with another man's child, or because she finds one who neglects or mistreats the child. But, in Darwinian terms, this cost is borne equally by the deserting husband; the child who will thus suffer is his child too, after all.

The big difference between men and women comes, rather, on the *benefits* side of the desertion ledger. What can each partner gain from a breakup in the way of future reproductive payoff? The husband can, in principle, find an eighteen-year-old woman with twenty-five years of reproduction ahead. The wife—even aside from the trouble she'll have finding a husband if she already has a child—cannot possibly find a mate who will give her twenty-five years worth of reproductive potential. This difference in outside opportunity is negligible at first, when both husband and wife are young. But as they age, it grows.

Circumstance can subdue or heighten it. A poor, low-status husband may not have a chance to desert and may, indeed, provide his wife with reason to desert, especially if she has no children and can thus find another mate readily. A husband who rises in status and wealth, on the other hand, will thus strengthen his incentive to desert while weakening his wife's. But all other things being equal, it is the husband's restlessness that will tend to grow as the years pass.

All this talk of "desertion" may be misleading. Though divorce is available in many hunter-gatherer cultures, so is polygyny; in the ancestral environment, gaining a second wife didn't necessarily mean leaving the first. And so long as it didn't, there was no good Darwinian reason to desert. Staying near offspring, giving protection and guidance, would have made more genetic sense. Thus, males may be designed less for opportune desertion than for opportune polygyny. But in the modern environment, with institutionalized monogamy, a polygynous impulse will find other outlets, such as divorce.

As a mother's children grow self-sufficient, the urgency of hang-

ing onto male parental investment drops. There are plenty of middle-aged women who, especially if they're financially secure, can take or leave their husbands. Still, there is no Darwinian force *driving* them to leave their husbands, nothing about leaving him that will sharply advance their genetic interests. The thing most likely to drive a post-menopausal woman out of a marriage is her husband's malicious marital discontent. Many a woman seeks divorce, but that doesn't mean *her* genes are ultimately the problem.

Among all the data on contemporary marriage, two items stand out as especially telling. First is the 1992 study which found that the husband's dissatisfaction with a marriage is the single strongest predictor of divorce.[66] Second is that men are much more likely than women to remarry after a divorce.[67] The second fact—and the biological force behind the second fact—is probably a good part of the reason for the first.

Objections to this sort of analysis are predictable: "But people leave marriages for *emotional* reasons. They don't add up the number of their children and pull out their calculators. Men are driven away by dull, nagging wives, or by the profound soul-searching of a mid-life crisis. Women are driven out by abusive or indifferent husbands, or lured away by a sensitive, caring man."

All true. But, again: emotions are just evolution's executioners. Beneath all the thoughts and feelings and temperamental differences that marriage counselors spend their time sensitively assessing are the stratagems of the genes—cold, hard equations composed of simple variables: social status, age of spouse, number of children, their ages, outside opportunities, and so on. Is the wife *really* duller and more nagging than she was twenty years ago? Possibly, but it's also possible that the husband's tolerance for nagging has dropped now that she's forty-five and has no reproductive future. And the promotion he just got, which has already drawn some admiring glances from a young woman at work, hasn't helped. Similarly, we might ask the young childless wife who finds her husband intolerably insensitive why the insensitivity wasn't so oppressive a year ago, before he lost his job and she met the kindly, affluent bachelor who seems to be flirting with her. Of course, maybe her husband's abuses are quite real, in which case they signal his disaffection, and perhaps his impending

departure—and merit just the sort of preemptive strike the wife is now mustering.

Once you start seeing everyday feelings and thoughts as genetic weapons, marital spats take on new meaning. Even the ones that aren't momentous enough to bring divorce are seen as incremental renegotiations of contract. The husband who on his honeymoon said he didn't want an "old-fashioned wife" now sarcastically suggests that it wouldn't be too taxing for her to cook dinner once in a while. The threat is as clear as it is implicit: I'm willing and able to break the contract if you're not willing to renegotiate.

PAIR BONDS REVISITED

All told, things are not looking good for Desmond Morris's version of the pair-bond hypothesis. We do not seem to be too much like our famously, just about unswervingly, monogamous primate relatives, the gibbons, to which we have been optimistically compared. This should come as no great surprise. Gibbons aren't very social. Each family lives on a large home range—sometimes more than a hundred acres—that buffers it from extramarital dalliances. And gibbons chase off any intruders that might want to steal or borrow a mate.[68] We, by contrast, have evolved in large social groups that are rife with genetically profitable alternatives to fidelity.

We do have, to be sure, the earmarks of high male parental investment. For hundreds of thousands of years, and maybe longer, natural selection has been inclining males to love their children, thus giving them a feeling females had been enjoying for the previous several hundred million years of mammalian evolution. Natural selection has also, during that time, been inclining men and women to love each other (or, at least, to "love" each other, with the meaning of that word varying greatly, and seldom approaching the constancy of devotion it reaches between parent and offspring). Still, love or no love, gibbons we aren't.

So what *are* we? Just how far from being naturally monogamous is our species? Biologists often answer this question anatomically. We've already seen anatomical evidence—testes weight and the fluctuations in sperm density—suggesting that human females are not devoutly monogamous by nature. There is also anatomical evidence bearing on the question of precisely how far from monogamous males naturally are. As Darwin noted, in highly polygynous species the contrast in body size between male and female—the "sexual dimorphism"—is great. Some males monopolize several females, while other males get shut out of the genetic sweepstakes altogether, so there is immense evolutionary value in being a big male, capable of intimidating other males. Male gorillas, who mate with lots of females if they win lots of fights and no females if they win none, are gargantuan—twice as heavy as females. Among the monogamous gibbons, small males breed about as prolifically as bigger ones, and sexual dimorphism is almost imperceptible. The upshot is that sexual dimorphism is a good index of the intensity of sexual selection among males, which in turn reflects how polygynous a species is. When placed on the spectrum of sexual dimorphism, humans get a "mildly polygynous" rating.[69] We're much less dimorphic than gorillas, a bit less than chimps, and markedly more than gibbons.

One problem with this logic is that competition among human, and even prehuman, males has been largely mental. Men don't have the long canine teeth that male chimps use to fight for alpha rank and thus supreme mating rights. But men do employ various stratagems to raise their social status, and thus their attractiveness. So some, and maybe much, of the polygyny in our evolutionary past would be reflected not in gross physiology but in distinctively male mental traits. If anything, the less than dramatic difference in size between men and women paints an overly flattering picture of men's monogamous tendencies.[70]

How have societies over the years coped with the basic sexual asymmetry in human nature? Asymmetrically. A huge majority— 980 of the 1,154 past or present societies for which anthropologists have data—have permitted a man to have more than one wife.[71] And that number includes most of the world's hunter-gatherer societies, societies that are the closest thing we have to a living example of the context of human evolution.

The more zealous champions of the pair-bond thesis have been known to minimize this fact. Desmond Morris, hell-bent on proving the natural monogamy of our species, insisted in *The Naked Ape* that the only societies worth paying much attention to are modern industrial societies, which, coincidentally, fall into the 15 percent of societies that have been avowedly monogamous. "[A]ny society that has failed to advance has in some sense failed, 'gone wrong,' " he wrote. "Something has happened to it to hold it back, something that is working against the natural tendencies of the species. . . . " So "the small, backward, and unsuccessful societies can largely be ignored." In sum, said Morris (who was writing back when Western divorce rates were about half what they are now): "whatever obscure, backward tribal units are doing today, the mainstream of our species expresses its pair-bonding character in its most extreme form, namely long-term monogamous matings."[72]

Well, that's one way to get rid of unsightly, inconvenient data: declare them aberrant, even though they vastly outnumber the "mainstream" data.

Actually, there *is* a sense in which polygynous marriage has not been the historical norm. For 43 percent of the 980 polygynous cultures, polygyny is classified as "occasional." And even where it is "common," multiple wives are generally reserved for a relatively few men who can afford them or qualify for them via formal rank. For eons and eons, most marriages have been monogamous, even though most societies haven't been.

Still, the anthropological record suggests that polygyny is natural in the sense that men given the opportunity to have more than one wife are strongly inclined to seize it. The record also suggests something else: that polygyny has its virtues as a way of handling the basic imbalance between what men and women want. In our culture, when a man whose wife has given him a few children grows restless and "falls in love" with a younger woman, we say: Okay, you can marry her, but we insist that you desert your first wife and that a stigma be placed on your kids and that, if you don't make much money, your kids and former wife suffer miserably. Some other cultures have tended to say: Okay, you can marry her, but only if you can really afford a second family; and you can't desert your first family, and there won't be any stigma placed on your kids.

Maybe some of today's nominally monogamous societies, those in which half of all marriages actually fail, should just go whole hog. Maybe we should fully erase the already fading stigma of divorce.

Maybe we should simply make sure that men who stray from their families remain legally responsible for them, and keep supporting them in the manner to which they had become accustomed. Maybe we should, in short, permit polygyny. A lot of presently divorced women, and their children, might be better off.

The only way to intelligently address this option is to first ask a simple question (one that turns out to have a counterintuitive answer): How did a strict cultural insistence on monogamy, which seems to go against the grain of human nature, and several millennia ago was almost unheard of, ever come to be?

Chapter 4: **THE MARRIAGE MARKET**

*It is hardly possible to read Mr. M'Lennan's work and not admit
that almost all civilised nations still retain some traces of such
rude habits as the forcible capture of wives. What ancient nation,
as the same author asks, can be named that was originally
monogamous?*

—*The Descent of Man* (1871)[1]

Something about the world doesn't seem to make sense. On the one
hand, it is run mostly by men. On the other hand, in most parts of
it, polygamy is illegal. If men really are the sort of animals described
in the two previous chapters, why did they let this happen?

Sometimes this paradox gets explained away as a compromise
between the male and female natures. In an old-fashioned, Victorian-
style marriage, men get routine subservience in exchange for keeping
their wanderlust more or less under control. The wives cook, clean,
take orders, and put up with all the unpleasant aspects of a regular
male presence. In return, the husbands graciously agree to stick
around.

This theory, however appealing, is beside the point. Granted,
within any monogamous marriage there is compromise. And within
any two-man prison cell there is compromise. But that doesn't mean
prisons were invented by a compromise among criminals. Compro-

mise between men and women is the way monogamy endures (when it does), but it's no explanation of how monogamy got here.

The first step toward answering the "Why monogamy" question is to understand that, for some monogamous societies on the anthropological record—including many hunter-gatherer cultures—the question isn't all that perplexing. These societies have hovered right around the subsistence level. In such a society, where little is stowed away for a rainy day, a man who stretches his resources between two families may end up with few or no surviving children. And even if he were willing to gamble on a second family, he'd have trouble attracting a second wife. Why should she settle for half of a poor man if she can have all of one? Out of love? But how often will love malfunction so badly? Its very purpose, remember, is to attract her to men who will be good for her progeny. Besides, why should her family—and in preindustrial societies families often shape a bride's "choice" forcefully and pragmatically—tolerate such foolishness?

Roughly the same logic holds if a society is somewhat above the subsistence level but all men are about equally above it. A woman who chooses half a husband over a whole one is still settling for much less in the way of material well-being.

The general principle is that economic equality among men—especially, but not only, if near the subsistence level—tends to short-circuit polygyny. This tendency by itself dispels a good part of the monogamy mystery, for more than half of the known monogamous societies have been classified as "nonstratified" by anthropologists.[2] What really demand explanation are the six dozen societies in the history of the world, including the modern industrial nations, that have been monogamous yet economically stratified. These are true freaks of nature.

The paradox of monogamy amid uneven affluence has been stressed especially by Richard Alexander, one of the first biologists to broadly apply the new paradigm to human behavior. When monogamy is found in subsistence-level cultures, Alexander calls it "ecologically imposed." When it appears in more affluent, more stratified cultures, he calls it "socially imposed."[3] The question is why society imposed it.

The term *socially imposed* may offend some people's romantic ideals. It seems to imply that, in the absence of bigamy laws, women would flock toward money, gleefully signing on as second or third wife so long as there was enough of it to go around. Nor is the term *flock* used lightly here. There is a tendency for polygyny to occur in bird species whose males control territories of sharply differing quality or quantity. Some female birds are quite happy to share a male so long as he has a lot more real estate than any male they could have monopolized.[4] Most human females would like to think they are guided by a more ethereal sort of love, and that they have somewhat more pride than a long-billed marsh wren.

And of course they do. Even in polygynous cultures, women are often less than eager to share a man. But, typically, they would rather do that than live in poverty with the undivided attention of a ne'er-do-well. It is easy for well-educated, upper-class women to scoff at the idea that any self-respecting woman would willingly suffer the degradation of polygyny, or to deny that women place great emphasis on a husband's income. But upper-class women seldom even *meet* a man with a low income, much less face the prospect of marrying one. Their milieu is so economically homogeneous that they don't have to worry about finding a minimally adequate provider; they can refocus their search, and spend their time pondering a prospective mate's taste in music and literature. (And these tastes are themselves cues to a man's socioeconomic status. This is a reminder that the Darwinian evaluation of a mate needn't be *consciously* Darwinian.)

In favor of Alexander's belief that there's something artificial about highly stratified yet monogamous societies is the fact that polygyny tends to lurk stubbornly beneath their surface. Though being a mistress is even today considered at least mildly scandalous, a number of women seem to prefer that role to the alternative: a greater commitment from a man of lesser means—or, perhaps, a commitment from no man.

Since Alexander began stressing the two kinds of monogamous societies, his distinction has drawn a second, more subtle, kind of support. The anthropologists Steven J. C. Gaulin and James S. Boster have shown that dowry—a transfer of assets from the bride's to the groom's family—is found almost exclusively in societies with socially imposed monogamy. Thirty-seven percent of these stratified nonpolygynous societies have had dowry, whereas 2 percent of all nonstratified nonpolygynous societies have. (For polygynous societies the figure is around 1 percent.)[5] Or, to put it another way: although only 7 percent of societies on record have had socially imposed monogamy, they account for 77 percent of societies with a dowry tradition. This suggests that dowry is the product of a market disequilibrium, a blockage of marital commerce; monogamy, by limiting each man to a single wife, makes wealthy men artificially precious commodities, and dowry is the price paid for them. Presumably, if polygyny were legalized, the market would right itself more straightforwardly: males with the most money (and perhaps with the most charm and the ruggedest physiques and whatever else might partly outweigh considerations of wealth) would, rather than fetch large dowries, have multiple wives.

WINNERS AND LOSERS

If we adopt this way of looking at things—if we abandon a Western ethnocentric perspective and hypothetically accept the Darwinian view that men (consciously or unconsciously) want as many sex-providing and child-making machines as they can comfortably afford, and women (consciously or unconsciously) want to maximize the resources available to their children—then we may have the key to explaining why monogamy is with us today: whereas a polygynous society is often depicted as something men would love and women would hate, there is really no natural consensus on the matter within either sex. Obviously, women who are married to a poor man and would rather have half of a rich one aren't well served by the institution of monogamy. And, obviously, the poor husband they would gladly desert wouldn't be well served by polygyny.

Nor are these superficially ironic preferences confined to people near the bottom of the income scale. Indeed, in sheerly Darwinian terms, *most* men are probably better off in a monogamous system and *most* women worse off. This is an important point, and warrants a brief illustrative detour.

Consider a crude and offensive but analytically useful model of the marital marketplace. One thousand men and one thousand women are ranked in terms of their desirability as mates. Okay, okay: there isn't, in real life, full agreement on such things. But there are clear patterns. Few women would prefer an unemployed and rudderless man to an ambitious and successful one, all other things being even roughly equal; and few men would choose an obese, unattractive, and dull woman over a shapely, beautiful, sharp one. For the sake of intellectual progress, let's simplemindedly collapse these and other aspects of attraction into a single dimension.

Suppose these 2,000 people live in a monogamous society and each woman is engaged to marry the man who shares her ranking. She'd like to marry a higher-ranking man, but they're all taken by competitors who outrank her. The men too would like to marry up, but for the same reason can't. Now, before any of these engaged couples gets married, let's legalize polygyny and magically banish its stigma. And let's suppose that at least one woman who is mildly more desirable than average—a quite attractive but not overly bright woman with a ranking of, say, 400—dumps her fiancé (male #400, a shoe salesman) and agrees to become the second wife of a successful lawyer (male #40). This isn't wildly implausible—forsaking a family income of around $40,000 a year, some of which she would have to earn herself by working part-time at a Pizza Hut, for maybe $100,000 a year and no job requirement (not to mention the fact that male #40 is a better dancer than male #400).[6]

Even this first trickle of polygynous upward mobility makes most women better off and most men worse off. All 600 women who ranked below the deserter move up one notch to fill the vacuum; they still get a husband all to themselves, and a better husband at that. Meanwhile 599 men wind up with a wife slightly inferior to their former fiancées—and one man now gets no wife at all. Granted: in real life, the women wouldn't move up in lockstep. Very early in the process, you'd find a woman who, pondering the various intangibles of attraction, would stand by her man. But in real life, you'd probably have more than a trickle of upward mobility in the first place. The basic point stands: many, many women, even many women *who will choose not to share a husband*, have their options expanded when all women are free to share a husband.[7] By the same token, many, many men can suffer at the hands of polygyny.

All told, then, institutionalized monogamy, though often viewed as a big victory for egalitarianism and for women, is emphatically not egalitarian in its effects on women. Polygyny would much more evenly distribute the assets of males among them. It is easy—and wise—for beautiful, vivacious wives of charming, athletic corporate titans to dismiss polygyny as a violation of the basic rights of women. But married women living in poverty—or women without a husband or child, and desirous of both—could be excused for wondering just which women's rights are protected by monogamy. The only under-privileged citizens who should favor monogamy are men. It is what gives them access to a supply of women that would otherwise drift up the social scale.

So neither gender, as a whole, belongs on either side of the im-aginary bargaining table that yielded the tradition of monogamy. Monogamy is neither a minus for men collectively nor a plus for women collectively; within both sexes, interests naturally collide. More plausibly, the grand, historic compromise was cut between more fortunate and less fortunate men. For them, the institution of monogamy does represent a genuine compromise: the most fortunate men still get the most desirable women, but they have to limit them-selves to one apiece. This explanation of monogamy—as a divvying up of sexual property among men—has the virtue of consistency with the fact that opened this chapter: namely, that it is men who usually control sheerly political power, and men who, historically, have cut most of the big political deals.

This is not to say, of course, that men ever sat down and ham-mered out the one-woman-per-man compromise. The idea, rather, is that polygyny has tended to disappear in response to egalitarian values—not values of equality between the sexes, but of equality among men. And maybe "egalitarian values" is too polite a way of putting it. As political power became distributed more evenly, the hoarding of women by upper-class men simply became untenable. Few things are more anxiety-producing for an elite governing class than gobs of sex-starved and childless men with at least a modicum of political power.

This thesis remains only a thesis.[8] But reality at least loosely fits it. Laura Betzig has shown that in preindustrial societies, extreme polygyny often goes hand in hand with extreme political hierarchy, and reaches its zenith under the most despotic regimes. (Among the Zulu, whose king might monopolize more than a hundred women, coughing, spitting, or sneezing at his dining table was punishable by death.) And the allocation of sexual resources by political status has often been fine-grained and explicit. In Inca society, the four political offices from petty chief to chief were allotted ceilings of seven, eight, fifteen, and thirty women, respectively.[9] It stands to reason that as political power became more widely disbursed, so did wives. And the ultimate widths are one-man-one-vote and one-man-one-wife. Both characterize most of today's industrialized nations.

Right or wrong, this theory of the origin of modern institutionalized monogamy is an example of what Darwinism has to offer historians. Darwinism does not, of course, explain history *as* evolution; natural selection doesn't work nearly fast enough to drive ongoing change at the level of culture and politics. But natural selection did shape the minds that *do* drive cultural and political change. And understanding how it shaped those minds may afford fresh insight into the forces of history. In 1985 the eminent social historian Lawrence Stone published an essay that stressed the epic significance of the early Christian emphasis on the fidelity of husbands and the permanence of marriage. After reviewing a couple of theories as to how this cultural innovation spread, he concluded that the answer "remains obscure."[10] Perhaps a Darwinian explanation—that, given human nature, monogamy is a straightforward expression of political equality among men—deserved at least a mention. It may be no accident that Christianity, which served as a vehicle for monogamy politically as well as intellectually, has often pitched its message to poor and powerless men.[11]

WHAT'S WRONG WITH POLYGYNY?

This Darwinian analysis of marriage complicates the choice between monogamy and polygyny. For it shows that the choice isn't between equality and inequality. The choice is between equality among men and equality among women. A tough call.

There are several conceivable reasons to vote for equality among men (that is, monogamy). One is to dodge the wrath of the various feminists who will not be convinced that polygyny liberates down-trodden women. Another is that monogamy is the only system that, theoretically at least, can provide a mate for just about everyone. But the most powerful reason is that leaving lots of men without wives and children is not just inegalitarian; it's dangerous.

The ultimate source of the danger is sexual selection among males. Men have long competed for access to the scarcer sexual resource, women. And the costs of losing the contest are so high (genetic oblivion) that natural selection has inclined them to compete with special ferocity. In all cultures, men wreak more violence, including murder, than women. (Indeed, across the animal kingdom, males are the more belligerent sex, *except* in those species, such as phalaropes, where male parental investment is so high females can reproduce more often than males.) Even when the violence isn't against a sexual rival, it often boils down to sexual competition. A trivial dustup may es-calate until one man kills another to "save face"—to earn the sort of raw respect that, in the ancestral environment, could have raised status and brought sexual rewards.[12]

Fortunately, male violence can be dampened by circumstance. And one circumstance is a mate. We would expect womanless men to compete with special ferocity, and they do. An unmarried man between twenty-four and thirty-five years of age is about three times as likely to murder another male as is a married man the same age. Some of this difference no doubt reflects the kinds of men that do and don't get married to begin with, but Martin Daly and Margo Wilson have argued cogently that a good part of the difference may lie in "the pacifying effect of marriage."[13]

Murder isn't the only thing an "unpacified" man is more likely to do. He is also more likely to incur various risks—committing robbery, for example—to gain the resources that may attract women. He is more likely to rape. More diffusely, a high-risk, criminal life often entails the abuse of drugs and alcohol, which may then com-pound the problem by further diminishing his chances of ever earning enough money to attract women by legitimate means.[14]

This is perhaps the best argument for monogamous marriage, with its egalitarian effects on men: inequality among males is more socially destructive—in ways that harm women *and* men—than inequality among women. A polygynous nation, in which large numbers of low-income men remain mateless, is not the kind of country many of us would want to live in.

Unfortunately, this is the sort of country we already live in. The United States is no longer a nation of institutionalized monogamy. It is a nation of serial monogamy. And serial monogamy in some ways amounts to polygyny.[15] Johnny Carson, like many wealthy, high-status males, spent his career monopolizing long stretches of the reproductive years of a series of young women. Somewhere out there is a man who wanted a family and a beautiful wife and, if it hadn't been for Johnny Carson, would have married one of these women. And if this man has managed to find another woman, she was similarly snatched from the jaws of some other man. And so on—a domino effect: a scarcity of fertile females trickles down the social scale.

As abstractly theoretical as this sounds, it really can't help but happen. There are only about twenty-five years of fertility per woman. When some men dominate more than twenty-five years' worth of fertility, some man, somewhere, must do with less. And when, on top of all the serial husbands, you add the young men who live with a woman for five years before deciding not to marry her, and then do it again (perhaps finally, at age thirty-five, marrying a twenty-eight-year-old), the net effect could be significant. Whereas in 1960 the fraction of the population age forty or older that had never married was about the same for men and women, by 1990 the fraction was markedly larger for men than for women.[16]

It is not crazy to think that there are homeless alcoholics and rapists who, had they come of age in a pre-1960s social climate, amid more equally distributed female resources, would have early on found a wife and adopted a lower-risk, less destructive lifestyle. Anyway, you don't have to buy this illustration to buy the point itself: if polygyny would indeed have pernicious effects on society's less fortunate men, and indirectly on the rest of us, then it isn't enough to just oppose legalized polygyny. (Legalized polygyny wasn't a looming political threat last time I checked, anyway.) We have to worry about the de facto polygyny that already exists. We have to ask not whether monogamy can be saved, but whether it can be restored. And we might be enthusiastically joined in this inquiry not only by discontented wifeless men, but by a large number of discontented former wives—especially the ones who had the bad fortune to marry someone less wealthy than Johnny Carson.

DARWINISM AND MORAL IDEALS

This view of marriage is a textbook example of how Darwinism can and can't legitimately enter moral discourse. What it can't do is furnish us with basic moral values. Whether, for example, we want to live in an egalitarian society is a choice for us to make; natural selection's indifference to the suffering of the weak is not something we need emulate. Nor should we care whether murder, robbery, and rape are in some sense "natural." It is for us to decide how abhorrent we find such things and how hard we want to fight them.

But once we've made such choices, once we *have* moral ideals, Darwinism can help us figure out which social institutions best serve them. In this case, a Darwinian outlook shows the prevailing marital institution, serial monogamy, to be in many ways equivalent to polygyny. As such, this institution is seen to have inegalitarian effects on men, working against the disadvantaged. Darwinism also highlights the costs of this inequality—violence, theft, rape.

In this light, old moral debates assume a new cast. For example, the tendency of political conservatives to monopolize the argument for "family values" starts to look odd. Liberals, concerned about the destitute, and about the "root causes" of crime and poverty, might logically develop a certain fondness for "family values." For a drop in the divorce rate, by making more young women accessible to low-income men, might keep an appreciable number of men from falling into crime, drug addiction, and, sometimes, homelessness.

Of course, given the material opportunities that polygyny (even de facto polygyny) may afford poor women, one can also imagine a liberal argument *against* monogamy. One can even imagine a liberal *feminist* argument against monogamy. And, in any event, one can see that a Darwinian feminism will be a more complicated feminism.

Viewed in Darwinian terms, "women" are not a naturally coherent interest group; there is no single sisterhood.[17]

There is one other kind of fallout from current marital norms that comes into focus through the new paradigm: the toll taken on children. Martin Daly and Margo Wilson have written, "Perhaps the most obvious prediction from a Darwinian view of parental motives is this: Substitute parents will generally tend to care less profoundly for children than natural parents." Thus, "children reared by people other than their natural parents will be more often exploited and otherwise at risk. Parental investment is a precious resource, and selection must favor those parental psyches that do not squander it on nonrelatives."[18]

To some Darwinians, this expectation might seem so strong as to render its verification a waste of time. But Daly and Wilson took the trouble. What they found surprised even them. In America in 1976, a child living with one or more substitute parents was about one hundred times more likely to be fatally abused than a child living with natural parents. In a Canadian city in the 1980s, a child two years of age or younger was seventy times more likely to be killed by a parent if living with a stepparent and natural parent than if living with two natural parents. Of course, murdered children are a tiny fraction of the children living with stepparents; the divorce and re-marriage of a mother is hardly a child's death warrant. But consider the more common problem of nonfatal abuse. Children under ten were, depending on their age and the particular study in question, between three and forty times more likely to suffer parental abuse if living with a stepparent and a natural parent than if living with two natural parents.[19]

It is fair to infer that many less dramatic, undocumented forms of parental indifference follow this rough pattern. After all, the whole reason natural selection *invented* paternal love was to bestow benefits on offspring. Though biologists call these benefits "investment," that doesn't mean they're strictly material, wholly sustainable through monthly checks. Fathers give their children all kinds of tutelage and guidance (more, often, than either father or child realizes) and guard them against all kinds of threats. A mother alone simply can't pick up the slack. A stepfather almost surely won't pick up much, if any of it. In Darwinian terms, a young stepchild is an obstacle to fitness, a drain on resources.

There are ways to fool mother nature, to induce parents to love children that aren't theirs. (Hence cuckoldry.) After all, people can't telepathically sense that a child is carrying their genes. Instead, they rely on cues that, in the ancestral environment, would have signified as much. If a woman feeds and cuddles an infant day after day, she may grow to love the child, and so may a man who has been sleeping with her for years. This sort of bonding is what makes adopted children lovable and nannies loving. But both theory and casual observation suggest that, the older a child is when first seen by the substitute parent, the less likely deep attachment is. And a large majority of children who acquire stepfathers are past infancy.

One can imagine arguments among reasonable and humane people over whether a strongly monogamous society is better than a strongly polygynous one. But this much seems less controversial: whenever marital institutions—in either kind of society—are allowed to dissolve, so that divorce and unwed motherhood are rampant, and many children no longer live with both natural parents, there will ensue a massive waste of the most precious evolutionary resource: love. Whatever the relative merits of monogamy and polygyny, what we have now—serial monogamy, de facto polygyny—is, in an important sense, the worst of all worlds.

PURSUING MORAL IDEALS

Obviously, Darwinism won't always simplify moral and political debate. In this case, by stressing the tension between equality among men and among women, it actually complicates the question of which marital institutions best serve our ideals. Still, the tension was always there; at least now it's in the open, and debate can proceed in stronger light. Further, once we *have* decided, with help from the new paradigm, which institutions best serve our moral ideals, Darwinism can make its second kind of contribution to moral discourse: it can help us figure out what sorts of forces—which moral norms, which social policies—help nourish those institutions.

And here comes another irony in the "family values" debate: conservatives may be surprised to hear that one of the best ways to strengthen monogamous marriage is to more equally distribute income.[20] Young single women will feel less inclined to tempt husband A away from wife A if bachelor B has just as much money. And husband A, if he's not drawing flirtatious looks from young women, may feel more content with wife A, and less inclined to notice her wrinkles. This dynamic presumably helps explain why monogamous marriage has often taken root in societies with little economic stratification.

One standard conservative argument against antipoverty policies is their cost: taxes burden the affluent and, by reducing their incentive to work, lower overall economic output. But if one goal of the policy is to bolster monogamy, then making the affluent less affluent is a welcome side effect. Monogamy is threatened not just by poverty in an absolute sense but also by the relative wealth of the wealthy. That reducing this wealth cuts overall economic output may, of course, still be regrettable; but once we add more stable marriages to the benefits of income redistribution, the regret should lose a bit of its sting.

One might imagine that this whole analysis is steadily losing its relevance. After all, as more women enter the workforce, they can better afford to premise their marital decisions on something other than the man's income. But remember: we're dealing with women's deep romantic attractions, not just their conscious calculation, and these feelings were forged in a different environment. To judge by hunter-gatherer societies, males during human evolution controlled most of the material resources. And even in the poorest of these societies, where disparities in male wealth are hard to detect, a father's social status often translates subtly into advantages for offspring, material and otherwise, in ways that a mother's social status doesn't.[21] Though a modern woman can of course reflect on her wealth and her independently earned status, and try to gauge marital decisions accordingly, that doesn't mean she can easily override the deep aesthetic impulses that had such value in the ancestral environment. In fact, modern women manifestly do not override them. Evolutionary psychologists have shown that the tendency of women to place greater emphasis than men on a mate's financial prospects persists regardless of the income or expected income of the women in question.[22]

So long as a society remains economically stratified, the challenge of reconciling lifelong monogamy with human nature will be large. Incentives and disincentives (moral and/or legal) may be necessary. One way to see what sorts of incentives can work is to look at an economically stratified society where they worked. Say, for example, Victorian England. To search for the peculiarities of Victorian morality that helped marriages succeed (at least in the minimal sense of not dissolving) isn't to say we should adopt those peculiarities ourselves. One can see the "wisdom" of some moral tenet—see how it achieves certain goals by implicitly recognizing deep truths about human nature—without finding it, on balance, worth the side effects. But seeing the wisdom is still a good way to appreciate the contours of the challenge it met. Looking at a Victorian marriage—Charles and Emma Darwin's—from a Darwinian point of view is worth the effort.

Before we return to Darwin's life, one caution is in order. So far we've been analyzing the human mind in the abstract; we've talked about "species-typical" adaptations designed to maximize fitness. When we shift our focus from the whole species to any one individual, we should *not* expect that person to chronically maximize fitness, to optimally convey his or her genes to future generations. And the reason goes beyond the one that has so far been stressed: that most human beings don't live in an environment much like the one for which their minds were designed. Environments—even the environments for which organisms *are* designed—are unpredictable. That is why behavioral flexibility evolved in the first place. And unpredictability, by its nature, cannot be mastered. As John Tooby and Leda Cosmides have put it, "Natural selection cannot directly 'see' an individual organism in a specific situation and cause behavior to be adaptively tailored."[23]

The best that natural selection can do is give us adaptations— "mental organs" or "mental modules"—that play the odds. It can give males a "love of offspring" module, and make that module sensitive to the likelihood that the offspring in question is indeed the man's. But the adaptation cannot be foolproof. Natural selection can give women an "attracted to muscles" module, or an "attracted to status" module, and, what's more, it can make the strength of those attractions depend on all kinds of germane factors; but even a highly flexible module can't guarantee that these attractions translate into viable and prolific offspring.

As Tooby and Cosmides say, human beings aren't general purpose "fitness maximizers." They are "adaptation executers."[24] The adaptations may or may not bring good results in any given case, and success is especially spotty in environments other than a small hunter-gatherer village. So as we look at Charles Darwin, the question isn't: Can we conceive of things he could have done to have more viable, prolific offspring than he had? The question is: Is his behavior intelligible as the product of a mind that consists of a bundle of adaptations?

Chapter 5: **DARWIN'S MARRIAGE**

Like a child that has something it loves beyond measure, I long to dwell on the words my own *dear Emma. . . . My own dear Emma, I kiss the hands with all humbleness and gratitude, which have so filled up for me the cup of happiness . . . but do dear Emma, remember life is short, and two months is the sixth part of the year.*

—Darwin in November 1838, in a letter to his fiancée,
urging an early wedding

Sexual desire makes saliva to flow . . . curious association.
—Darwin in his scientific notebook, same month, same year[1]

In the decade of Darwin's marriage, the 1830s, the number of British couples filing for divorce averaged four per year. This is in some ways a misleading statistic. It probably reflects, in part, the tendency of men back then to die before reaching the climax of their midlife crises. (A misnomer; often the wife's middle age, more than the man's, brings on the crisis.) And it certainly reflects the fact that getting a divorce required—literally—an act of Parliament. Marriages also ended in other ways, especially through privately arranged separations. Still, there's no denying that marriage back then was, by and large, for keeps, especially within Darwin's upper-middle-class social stratum. And marriage stayed that way for half a century after 1857, the year the Divorce Act made breaking up easier to do.[2] There was something about Victorian morality conducive to staying married.

There is no telling how much misery was generated in Victorian England by unhappy, unendable marriages. But it may well not exceed the misery generated by modern marital dissolution.[3] In any case, we do know of some Victorian marriages that seem to have been successful. Among these is the marriage of Charles and Emma Darwin. Their devotion was mutual and seems, if anything, to have strengthened with time. They created seven children who lived to adulthood, and none of them penned nasty memoirs about tyrannical parents ("Darwin Dearest"). Their daughter Henrietta called their marriage a "perfect union."[4] Their son Francis wrote of his father: "In his relationship towards my mother, his tender and sympathetic nature was shown in its most beautiful aspect. In her presence he found his happiness, and through her, his life,—which might have been overshadowed by gloom,—became one of content and quiet gladness."[5] Viewed from today, the marriage of Charles and Emma Darwin appears almost idyllic in its geniality, tranquility, and sheer durability.

DARWIN'S PROSPECTS

On the Victorian marriage market, Darwin must have been a fairly desirable commodity. He had a winning disposition, a respectable education, a family tradition that augured well for his career, and, in any event, his looming inheritance. He wasn't notably handsome, but so what? The Victorians were very clear about their division of aesthetic labor, and it was consistent with evolutionary psychology: good financial prospects made for an attractive husband, and good looks made for an attractive wife. In the large correspondence between Darwin and his sisters—while he was at college, or, later, on the *Beagle*—there is much talk of romance, as his sisters report gossip and relay any reconnaissance work they've done on his behalf. Almost invariably, men are gauged by their ability to provide materially for a woman, while women are seen as providing a pleasant visual and auditory environment for a man. Newly betrothed women, and the women who qualify as prospects for Charles, are "pretty" or "charming" or, at the very least, "pleasant." "I am sure you would like her," Charles's sister Catherine wrote of one candidate. "She is so very merry and pleasant, and I think very pretty." Newly betrothed men, on the other hand, are either of means or not of means. Susan Darwin wrote to her brother during his voyage: "Your charming Cousin Lucy Galton is engaged to marry Mr. Moilliet: the eldest son of a *very fat* Mrs. Moilliet. . . . The young Gentleman has a good fortune, so of course the match gives great satisfaction."[6]

The *Beagle*'s voyage lasted longer than expected, and Darwin wound up spending five years—the heart of his twenties—away from England. But, like undistinguished looks, advancing age was something men didn't have to worry greatly about. Women of Darwin's class often spent their early twenties on prominent display, hoping to catch a man while in their prime. Men often spent their twenties as Darwin did—singlemindedly pursuing the sort of professional stature (and/or money) that might later attract a woman in her prime. There was no rush. It was considered natural for a woman to marry a markedly older man, whereas a Victorian man who married a much older woman was cause for dismay. While Darwin was aboard the *Beagle*, his sister Catherine reported that cousin Robert Wedgwood, who was around Darwin's age, had "fallen vehemently and desperately in love with Miss Crewe, who is 50 years old, and blind of one eye." His sister Susan chimed in sarcastically, "just 20 years difference in their ages!" And sister Caroline: "a woman more than old enough to be his Mother." Catherine had a theory: "She is a clever woman, and must have entrapped him by her artifices; & she has the remains of great beauty to help her."[7] In other words: the man's age-detection system was functioning as designed, but he happened upon a woman whose enduring beauty—that is, youthful appearance—fooled it.

The realm within which the young Darwin was likely to find a mate was not vast. From adolescence on, the likely candidates came from two well-to-do families not far from the Darwin home in Shrewsbury. There was the ever-popular Fanny Owen—"the prettiest, plumpest, Charming" Fanny Owen, as Darwin described her during college.[8] And then there were the three youngest daughters of Josiah Wedgwood II, Darwin's maternal uncle: Charlotte, Fanny, and Emma.[9]

As of the *Beagle*'s departure, no one seems to have picked Emma as the frontrunner for Charles's affections—though his sister Caroline, in a letter sent to him around then, did note in passing that "Emma is looking very pretty & chats very pleasantly."[10] (What more could a man ask for?) As fate would have it, the other three candidates dropped out of the running in short order.

First to go was Emma's sister Charlotte. In January of 1832, she wrote Darwin to announce her unexpected engagement to a man who, she admitted, had "only a very small income now" but stood to inherit much upon his grandmother's death, and, anyway, had "high principles & kind nature which gives me a feeling of security. . . ."[11] (Translation: resources in the offing, and a reliable willingness to invest them parentally.) Charlotte had, in truth, probably been a dark horse as far as Charles was concerned. Though she had impressed both him and his brother Erasmus—they referred to her as "the incomparable"—she was more than a decade older than Charles; Erasmus was probably more smitten by her (as he seems to have been by a series of women, none of whom he managed to marry).

More unsettling than Charlotte's fate, probably, was the almost simultaneous news that the beguiling Fanny Owen was also to take the plunge. Fanny's father wrote to Charles of the news, plainly disappointed that the groom was "now not very rich & indeed probably never will be."[12] On the other hand, her husband was a man of status, serving briefly in Parliament.

Darwin, responding to all this matrimonial news in a letter to his sister Caroline, made no pretense of happiness. "Well it may be all very delightful to those concerned, but as I like unmarried women better than those in the blessed state, I vote it a bore."[13]

The vision that Darwin's sisters had of his future—becoming a country parson and settling down with a good wife—was not growing more likely as potential wives fell by the wayside. Catherine surveyed the remains, Emma and Fanny Wedgwood, and gave the nod to Fanny. She wrote to Charles that she hoped Fanny would still be single when he returned—"a nice little invaluable Wife she would be."[14] We'll never know. She fell ill and died within a month, at age twenty-six. With three of the four contenders either married or buried, the odds shifted decisively in Emma's favor.

If Charles had long-standing designs on Emma, he hid them well. He had predicted, as Catherine recalled, that upon his return he would find Erasmus "tied neck and heels to Emma Wedgwood, and heartily sick of her." In 1832, Catherine wrote to Charles that "I am much amused at your prophecy, and I think it may possibly have a good effect, and prevent its own fulfillment."[15] Erasmus continued to show interest in Emma, but she was still available when the *Beagle* returned to England in 1836. In fact, you might say she was emphatically available. She had been a carefree twenty-three when the *Beagle* set sail, and over the next couple of years had gotten several marriage proposals. But now she was a year and a half from thirty and spending much time at home caring for her invalid mother; she wasn't getting quite the exposure she had once gotten.[16] In preparation for Darwin's arrival, she wrote to her sister-in-law, she was reading a book on South America "to get up a little knowledge for him."[17]

There was cause to wonder whether "a little knowledge" would be enough to keep Charles's attention focused on childhood friends. Upon returning, he possessed something that women in all cultures and at all times seem to have prized in men: status. He had always had high social standing by virtue of his family's rank, but now he had a prominence all his own. From the *Beagle*, Darwin had sent back fossils, organic specimens, and acute observations on geology that had won a large scientific audience. He now rubbed elbows with the great naturalists of the day. By the spring of 1837, he had settled into London, in bachelor's quarters a few doors down from his brother Erasmus, and was in social demand.

A person of greater vanity and less certain purpose might have been drawn into a time-sapping social whirl—a corruption that the gregarious Erasmus would have been delighted to abet. Certainly Darwin was aware of his growing stature ("I was quite a lion there," he reported of a visit to Cambridge). But he was too measured and earnest a man to be a mingler by nature. As often as not, he saw fit to forgo large gatherings. He would, he told his mentor, Professor John Henslow, "prefer paying you a quiet visit to meeting all the world at a great Dinner." A note of demurral to Charles Babbage, the mathematician who designed the "analytical engine," forerunner of the digital computer, began, "My dear Mr. Babbage, I am very much obliged to you for sending me cards for your parties, but I am afraid of accepting them, for I should meet some people there, to whom I have sworn by all the saints in Heaven, I never go out. . . ."[18]

With the time thus saved, Darwin embarked on a remarkable burst of accomplishment. Within two years of his return to England, he: (1) edited his shipboard journal into a publishable volume (which reads nicely, sold well, and is today in print, further abridged, under the title *Voyage of the Beagle*); (2) skillfully extracted a thousand-pound subsidy from the Chancellor of the Exchequer for publication of *The Zoology of the Voyage of H.M.S. Beagle* and lined up contributors to it; (3) consolidated his place in British science by presenting half a dozen papers, ranging from a sketch of a new species of American ostrich (named *Rhea darwinii* by the Zoological Society of London) to a new theory about the formation of topsoil ("every particle of earth forming the bed from which the turf in old pasture land springs, has passed through the intestines of worms");[19] (4) went on a geological expedition to Scotland; (5) hobnobbed with eminences at the exclusive men's club the Athenaeum; (6) was elected secretary of the Geological Society of London (a post he accepted reluctantly, fearing its demand on his time); (7) compiled scientific notebooks—on subjects ranging from the "species question" to religion to human moral faculties—of such high intellectual density that they would serve as the basis for his largest works in the ensuing four decades; and (8) thought up the theory of natural selection.

CHOOSING MARRIAGE

It was toward the end of this phase—a few months before natural selection dawned on him—that Darwin decided to marry. Not necessarily anyone in particular; it isn't clear that he had Emma Wedgwood even remotely in mind, and one common view is that she wasn't at the center of his thinking on the subject. In a remarkable deliberative memorandum, apparently composed around July of 1838, he decided the matter of marriage in the abstract.

The document has two columns, one labeled *Marry*, one labeled *Not Marry*, and above them, circled, are the words "This is the Question." On the pro-marriage side of the equation were "Children—(if it Please God)—Constant companion, (&friend in old age) who will feel interested in one,—object to be beloved & played with."

After reflection of unknown length, he modified the foregoing sentence with "better than a dog anyhow." He continued: "Home, & someone to take care of house— Charms of music & female chit-chat— These things good for one's health.— *but terrible loss of time*." Without warning, Darwin had, from the pro-marriage column, swerved uncontrollably into a major anti-marriage factor, so major that he underlined it. This issue—the infringement of marriage on his time, especially his work time—was addressed at greater length in the appropriate, *Not Marry* column. Not marrying, he wrote, would preserve "Freedom to go where one like—choice of Society & *little of it*.—Conversation of clever men at clubs—not forced to visit relatives, & to bend in every trifle—to have the expense & anxiety of children—Perhaps quarelling—*Loss of time*.—cannot read in the Evenings—fatness & idleness—Anxiety & responsibility— less money for books &c—if many children forced to gain one's bread."

Yet the pro-marriage forces carried the day, with this train of thought at the end of the *Marry* column: "My God, it is intolerable to think of spending ones whole life, like a neuter bee, working, working, & nothing after all.—No, no won't do.—Imagine living all one's day solitarily in smoky dirty London House.—Only picture to yourself a nice soft wife on a sofa with good fire, & books & music perhaps." After recording these images he wrote: "Marry-Mary[sic]-Marry Q.E.D."

Darwin's decision had to survive one more wave of doubt. The backlash began innocently enough, as Darwin wrote, "It being proved necessary to Marry, When? Soon or Late." But this question incited that final spasm of panic with which many grooms are familiar. Brides are familiar with it too, of course, but their doubt seems more often to be whether their choice of a lifelong mate is the right one. For men, as Darwin's memo attests, the panic isn't essentially related to any particular prospective mate; it is the *concept* of a lifelong mate that is at some level frightening. For—in a monogamous society, at least—it dampens the prospects for intimacy with all those other women that a man's genes urge him to find and get to know (however briefly).

This isn't to say that the premarital panic fixes itself coarsely on images of would-be sex partners; the subconscious can be more subtle than that. Still, there is, somewhat reliably among men who are about to pledge themselves to one woman for life, a dread of impending entrapment, a sense that the days of adventure are over. "Eheu!!" Darwin wrote, with one final shudder in the face of lifelong commitment. "I never should know French,—or see the Continent—or go to America, or go up in a Balloon, or take solitary trip in Wales—poor slave—you will be worse than a negro." But then, fatefully, he mustered the necessary resolve. "Never mind my boy—Cheer up—One cannot live this solitary life, with groggy old age, friendless & cold, & childless staring one in ones face, already beginning to wrinkle.—Never mind, trust to chance—keep a sharp look out—There is many a happy slave—" End of document.[20]

CHOOSING EMMA

Darwin had written an earlier deliberative memorandum, probably in April, in which he rambled on about career paths—teach at Cambridge? in geology? in zoology? or "Work at transmission of Species"?—and pondered the marriage question inconclusively.[21] There is no way of knowing what drove him to reopen the question and this time settle it. But it's intriguing that, of the six entries made between April and July in his sporadically kept personal journal, two say he was feeling "unwell." Unwellness was to become a way of life for Darwin, a fact he may already have suspected. It is ironic that hints of mortality can draw a man into marriage, for often it is these same hints, much later, that drive him out, to seek fresh proof of his virility. But the irony dissolves when reduced to ultimate cause: both the impulses to profess lifelong love to a woman and to wander lie within a man by virtue of how often, in his ancestors, they led to progeny. In that sense, both are an apt antidote to mortality, though in the end futile (except from the genes' point of view), and, in the latter case—wandering—often destructive as well.

Anyway, on a less philosophical plane: Darwin may have sensed that he would before long need a devoted helpmate and nurse. And perhaps he even had a glimmer of spending many years working, in patient and needy solitude, on a big book about evolution. As Darwin's health had gotten worse, his grasp of that subject had gotten better. He opened his first notebook on "transmutation of Species" in June or July of 1837, and his second in early 1838.[22] By the time he was rigorously mulling marriage, he had gone some of the way toward natural selection. He believed that one key to evolution lay in initially slight hereditary difference; that when a species is divided into two populations by, say, a body of water, what are at first merely two variants of the species grow apart until they qualify as new and distinct species.[23] All that remained—the hard part—was to figure out what guided that divergence. In July of 1838, he finished his second species notebook and opened his third, the one that would bring him the answer. And he may, as he penned his fateful marriage memorandum that same month, have had a sense of impending success.

In late September, the solution came. Darwin had just read Thomas Malthus's famous essay on population, which noted that a human population's natural rate of growth will tend to outstrip the food supply unless checked. Darwin recalled in his autobiography: "[B]eing well prepared to appreciate the struggle for existence which everywhere goes on from long-continued observation of the habits of animals and plants, it at once struck me that under these circumstances favourable variations would tend to be preserved, and unfavourable ones to be destroyed. The result of this would be the formation of new species. Here, then, I had at last got a theory by which to work."[24] Under the heading of September 28, Darwin jotted in his notebook some lines about Malthus and then, without explicitly describing natural selection, surveyed its effects: "One may say there is a force like a hundred thousand wedges trying [to] force every kind of adapted structure into the gaps in the economy of Nature, or rather forming gaps by thrusting out weaker ones. The final cause of all this wedgings, must be to sort out proper structure & adapt it to change."[25]

The direction of Darwin's professional life was set, and now he fixed the course of his personal life. Six weeks after writing this passage, on Sunday, November 11 ("The Day of Days!" he wrote in his personal journal), he proposed to Emma Wedgwood.

Viewed in the simplest Darwinian terms, Darwin's attraction to Emma seems strange. He was now a high-status and well-to-do man in his late twenties. Presumably he could have had a young and beautiful wife. Emma was a year older than he and, though not unattractive (at least in the eyes of her portrait painter), was not thought beautiful. Why would Darwin do anything so maladaptive as to marry a plain woman who had already exhausted more than a decade of her reproductive potential?

First of all, this simple equation—rich, high-status male equals young, beautiful wife—is a bit crude. There are many factors that make for a genetically auspicious mate, including intelligence, trustworthiness, and various sorts of compatibility.[26] Moreover, the selection of a spouse is also the selection of a parent for one's offspring. Emma's sturdiness of character foreshadowed the attentiveness she would bring to her children. One of her daughters recalled: "Her sympathy, and the serenity of her temper, made her children feel absolutely at their ease with her, and sure of comfort in every trouble great or small, whilst her unselfishness made them know that she would never find anything a burden, and that they could go to her with all the many little needs of a child for help or explanation."[27]

Besides, if the issue is how "valuable" a wife Darwin should be expected to seek, the question isn't, strictly speaking, how marketable a mate he was, but how marketable he had been given the impression he was. By adolescence, if not earlier, people are getting feedback about their market value, feedback that shapes their self-esteem and thus affects how high they aim their sights. Darwin doesn't seem to have emerged from adolescence feeling like an alpha male. Though large, he was meek, not much of a fighter. And, as one of his daughters noted, he considered his face "repellently plain."[28]

Of course, all of this was rendered less relevant by later achievement. Darwin may not have had high status as a teenager, but he got it later, and status per se can compensate, in the eyes of women, for mediocre looks and a lack of brute strength. Yet his insecurity seems to have persisted—as, indeed, insecurities formed in adolescence often do. The question is why.

Maybe the developmental mechanism that fine-tuned Darwin's insecurity was a vestige of evolution, an adaptation that would have tended to raise fitness in the ancestral environment but no longer does. In many hunter-gatherer societies, the male dominance hier-

who will send me to my lessons, and make me better, I trust, in every respect. . . ."[34]

DARWIN GETS EXCITED

To say that Darwin carefully and rationally selected his wife isn't to say that he wasn't in love with her. By the time of their wedding day, his letters to Emma were so laden with emotion as to raise a question: How did his feelings accelerate so rapidly? As of July, he is, depending on your interpretation of the evidence, either (a) not even dreaming of marrying her in particular; or (b) dithering violently over whether to marry her. In late July, he pays her a visit, and they have a long talk. On his next visit, three and a half months later, he pops the question. Now, suddenly, he is in ecstasy, writing florid letters about how he waits anxiously for the day's mail in the hope it will hold a letter from her; how he lies awake at night thinking of their future together; how "I long for the day when we shall enter the house together; how glorious it will be to see you seated by the fire of our own house."[35] What has happened to this man?

At the risk of seeming to harp on a single theme, I direct your attention again to the subject of genes. In particular: the differing genetic interests of a man and a woman who have never had sex with one another. Pre-sex, a woman's genes often call for wary evaluation. Affection should not too quickly become overwhelming passion. The male's genetic interest, meanwhile, often lies in speeding things up, saying things that will melt the woman's reserve. High on the list of these things are intimations of deep affection and eternal devotion. And nothing produces more convincing intimations then *feelings* of affection and devotion.

This logic may be amplified by various circumstances, and one of them is how much sex the man has been getting up until now. As Martin Daly and Margo Wilson have observed, "any creature that is recognizably on track toward complete reproductive failure" should, in theory, try with increasing intensity to change this trajectory.[36] That is: natural selection probably would not have been kind to the genes of men whose quest for sex wasn't accelerated by its prolonged absence. So far as anyone knows, Darwin went through his bachelor years without ever having sexual intercourse.[37] How little does it take to arouse a man who has been so long deprived? When the *Beagle* docked in Peru, Darwin saw elegant ladies shrouded in veils that exposed only one eye. "But then," he wrote, "that one eye is so black and brilliant and has such powers of motion and expression that its effect is very powerful."[38] It is not surprising that when Emma Wedgwood was placed within reach—her whole face visible, and her body soon to be his—Darwin began to salivate. (Literally, it would seem. See Darwin's journal excerpt at the head of this chapter.)

It is hard to estimate the exact ratio of love to lust in Darwin's heart as the wedding approached; their relative reproductive value during our evolutionary past has varied widely from moment to moment (as it still does) and from millennium to millennium. A few weeks before the wedding, Darwin mused in one of his scientific notebooks, "What passes in a man's mind when he says he loves a person . . . it is blind feeling, something like sexual feelings—love being an emotion does it regard—is it influenced by—other emotions?"[39] Like many passages in Darwin's notebooks, this is cryptic, but in mentioning love and sexual feelings in the same breath, and in suggesting that love may be subterraneanly rooted in other feelings, it seems headed in the general direction of a modern Darwinian view of human psychology. And it suggests (as does his mention of salivation) that he was, at that point, experiencing more than one kind of feeling toward Emma.

What was Emma feeling? If indeed the male's intense interest in impending sex is often matched by lingering female wariness, she might be expected to feel somewhat less ardor than Darwin. There are all kinds of factors that could change things in any one case, of course, but this is the generic expectation: more female than male ambivalence about consummation. Thus the Victorian postponement of sex until marriage should theoretically have shifted power toward women during the engagement. While the man had cause to be eager for the wedding day (compared to today's men, at least), the woman had cause to pause and reflect (compared to today's women, at least).

Emma complied with theory. Weeks into the engagement, she suggested that the wedding be put off until spring, whereas Darwin was pushing for winter. She cited the feelings of her sister Sarah Elizabeth, who, fifteen years her senior and still unwed, had mixed emotions about the event. But Emma added candidly, in a letter to Darwin's sister Catherine, "besides which I should wish it myself." She urged, "Do dear Catty clog the wheels a little slow."[40]

Darwin, enlisting some lush prose ("hope deferred does make my heart quite sick to call you in truth my wife"), kept the honeymoon from receding. But even after the wedding date was firm, he seems to have been left a bit insecure by Emma's reluctance, and perhaps by her overall tenor; her letters are warm, but they're far from effusive. Darwin wrote: "I earnestly pray, you may never regret the great, & I will add very good, deed, you are to perform on *the* Tuesday." Emma tried to reassure him, but she wasn't under the same magical spell he was under: "You need not fear my own dear Charles that I shall not be quite as happy as you are & I shall always look upon the event of the 29th as a most happy one on my part though perhaps not so great or so good as you do."[41] Ouch.

Now, all of this may reflect wholly on the peculiar dynamics between Charles and Emma, and not at all on the Victorian linkage of marriage with consummation. Emma was never an overly sentimental woman.[42] And, anyway, she may have begun having doubts about Charles's health, doubts that would have been warranted. Still, the basic point is probably valid in the aggregate: if it is harder to drag men to the altar today than it used to be, one reason is that they don't have to stop there on the way to the bedroom.

AFTER THE HONEYMOON

Consummation can alter the balance of affection. Though the average woman is more selective in unleashing her ardor than the average man, she should, in theory, be less inclined to rein it in once it has left the gate. Having deemed a man worthy of joining in her epic parental investment, she typically has a strong genetic interest in keeping him involved. Again, Emma's behavior matches expectations. Within the first few months of their marriage she wrote: "I cannot tell him how happy he makes me and how dearly I love him and thank him for all his affection which makes the happiness of my life more and more every day."[43]

Whether a man's devotion will be nourished by consummation is a less certain matter. Maybe his professions of affection were self-delusion; maybe, once his mate is pregnant, a better deal will come along. But in Darwin's case, the early signs were good. Months after his wedding day (and weeks after the conception of his first child), Darwin, writing in his notebook, groped for an evolutionary explanation of why a man's acts of "kindness to wife and children would give him pleasure, without any regard to his own interest," which suggests that his affection for Emma still felt deep.[44]

Perhaps this is not surprising. The tactical value of a woman's sexual reserve isn't just that men desperately want sex and to get it may say anything, even *believe* anything—including "I want to spend my whole life with you." If a Madonna-whore switch is indeed built into the male brain, then a woman's early reticence can lastingly affect a man's view of her. He is more likely to respect her in the morning—and perhaps for many years to come—if she doesn't weaken under his advances. He may *say* "I love you" to various women he yearns for, and he may mean it; but he may be more likely to keep meaning it if he doesn't get them right away. There may have been a bit of wisdom in the Victorian disapproval of premarital sex.

Even beyond this disapproval, Victorian culture was finely calibrated to excite the "Madonna" part of a man's mind and numb the "whore" part. The Victorians themselves called their attitude toward females "woman worship." The woman was a redeemer—innocence and purity incarnate; she could tame the animal in a man and rescue his spirit from the deadening world of work. But she could only do this in a domestic context, under the blessing of marriage, and after a long, chaste courtship. The secret was to have, as the title of one Victorian poem put it, an "Angel in the House."[45]

The idea wasn't just that men were supposed to at some point quit sowing wild oats, get hitched, and worship their wives. They were supposed to not sow the wild oats in the first place. Though the double standard for promiscuity prevailed in nineteenth-century Britain as elsewhere, it was battled by the more austere guardians of

Victorian morality (including Dr. Acton), who preached not just extramarital, but also premarital, abstinence for men. In *The Victorian Frame of Mind* Walter Houghton writes, "To keep body and mind untainted, the boy was taught to view women as objects of the greatest respect and even awe." Though he was supposed to give all women this respect, a certain kind of woman warranted something more. "He was to consider nice women (like his sister and his mother, like his future bride) as creatures more like angels than human beings— an image wonderfully calculated not only to dissociate love from sex, but to turn love into worship, and worship of purity."[46]

When Houghton says "calculated," he means it. One author in 1850 expressed the virtue of male premarital chastity as follows: "Where should we find that reverence for the female sex, that tenderness towards the feelings, that deep devotion of the heart to them, which is the beautiful and purifying part of love? Is it not certain that all of [the] delicate and chivalric which still pervades our sentiments towards women, may be traced to *repressed*, and therefore hallowed and elevated passion? . . . And what, in these days, can preserve chastity, save some relic of chivalrous devotion? Are we not all aware that a young man can have no safeguard against sensuality and low intrigue, like an early, virtuous, and passionate attachment?"[47]

Aside from the word *repressed*, which probably mischaracterizes the psychodynamics, this passage is plausible enough. It implies that a man's passion can be "hallowed and elevated" if not quenched too readily—that a chaste courtship, in other words, helps move a woman into the "Madonna" part of his mind.

This is not the only reason that a chaste courtship may encourage marriage. Recall how different the ancestral environment was from the modern environment. In particular: there were no condoms, diaphragms, or birth-control pills. So if an adult couple paired up, slept together for a year or two, and produced no baby, the chances were good that one of them wasn't fertile. No way of telling which one, of course; but for both of them there was little to lose and much to gain by dissolving the partnership and finding a new mate. The adaptation expected to arise from this logic is a "mate-ejection module"—a mental mechanism, in both male and female, that would encourage souring on a mate after lots of sex without issue.[48]

This is a quite speculative theory, but it has some circumstantial evidence on its side. In cultures around the world, barren marriages are among the most likely to break up.[49] (Though cases where barrenness is cited as the cause of breakup don't quite get at the crux of this theory: the *unconsciously* motivated alienation from a mate.) And, as many husbands and wives can attest, the birth of a child often cements a marital bond, if obliquely; the love of spouse is partly diverted to the child and then refracted diffusely onto the family as a whole, mate included. It is a different *kind* of love for the spouse, but it's sturdy in its own way. In the absence of this roundabout recharge, love of spouse may tend to disappear entirely—by design.

Darwin once worried that contraceptive technology would "spread to unmarried women & would destroy chastity on which the family bond depends; & the weakening of this bond would be the greatest of all possible evils to mankind."[50] He surely didn't grasp all the plausible Darwinian reasons that contraception and the attendant premarital sex might indeed discourage marriage. He didn't suspect the deep basis of the Madonna-whore dichotomy or the possible existence of a "mate-ejection module." And even today, we're far from certain about these things. (The established correlations between premarital sex and divorce, and between premarital cohabitation and divorce, are suggestive but ambiguous.)[51] Still, it is harder now than it would have been thirty years ago to dismiss Darwin's fear as the rantings of an aging Victorian.

Contraception isn't the only technology that may affect the structure of family life. Women who breast-feed often report a weakened sex drive—and with good Darwinian cause, since they're usually incapable of conception. Husbands, meanwhile, sometimes fail to find a breast-feeding wife sexually exciting, presumably for the same ultimate reason. Thus bottle-feeding may make wives both more lustful and more attractive. Whether this is, on balance, good for family cohesion is hard to say. (Does it more often tempt wives into extramarital affairs or distract husbands from having them?) In any event, this logic may make sense of Dr. Acton's otherwise comical-sounding claim that "the best mothers, wives, and managers of house-holds, know little or nothing of sexual indulgences. Love of home, children, and domestic duties, are the only passions they feel." In Victorian England, when so many wives spent so many of their fertile years either pregnant or nursing, their passion may indeed have spent much time in abeyance.[52]

Even if a succession of babies helps keep both partners devoted, the interests of husband and wife may diverge as time goes by. The older the children (the less urgently needful of paternal investment), and the older the wife, the less support a man's devotion gets from his evolutionary heritage. More and more of the harvest has been reaped; the ground is less and less fertile; it may be time to move on.[53] Of course, whether the husband feels this impulse strongly may depend on how likely it is to bear fruit. A dashing and wealthy man may get the kinds of glances from women that fuel it; a poor and disfigured man may not. Still, the strength of the impulse will tend to be greater in the husband than in the wife.

Though the shifting balance of attraction between husband and wife is seldom described this explicitly, it is often reflected more obliquely—in novels, in aphorisms, in the folk wisdom offered up as advice to bride and groom. Professor Henslow, a fifteen-year veteran of the blessed state, wrote to Darwin shortly before his mar-riage: "All the advice, which I need not give you, is, to remember that as you take your wife for better for worse, be careful to value the better & care nothing for the worse." He added: "It is the neglect of this little particular which makes the marriage state of so many men worse than their single blessedness."[54] In other words, just re-member one simple rule: don't stop loving your wife, as men seem inclined to do.

Emma, meanwhile, was getting advice not about overlooking Charles's flaws, but about concealing any flaws of her own, especially those that make a woman look old and haggard. An aunt (perhaps mindful of Emma's noted lack of fashion consciousness) wrote: "If you do pay a little more, be always dressed in good taste; do not despise those little cares which give everyone more pleasing looks, because you know you have married a man who is above caring for such little things. No man is above caring for them. . . . I have seen it even in my half-blind husband."[55]

The logic of male intolerance typically remains opaque to all concerned. A man souring on a mate doesn't think, "My reproductive potential is best served by getting out of this marriage, so for entirely selfish reasons I'll do so." Awareness of his selfishness would only impede its pursuit. It's much simpler for the feelings that got him into the marriage to simply stage a slow but massive retreat.

The increasingly severe view that a restless husband may take of an aging wife was well illustrated by Charles Dickens, one of the few upper-class Victorians who actually got out of a marriage (by separation, not divorce). Dickens, who was elected to membership in London's Athenaeum Club on the same day in 1838 as Darwin, had then been married for two years to the woman he called his "better half." Two decades later—now much more famous, and thus commanding the attention of many young women—he was having trouble seeing her brighter side. It now seemed to him that she lived in a "fatal atmosphere which slays every one to whom she should be dearest." Dickens wrote to a friend: "I believe that no two people were ever created with such an impossibility of interest, sympathy, confidence, sentiment, tender union of any kind between them, as there is between my wife and me." (If so, mightn't he have discussed this with her *before* she bore him ten children?) "To his eyes," a chronicler of their marriage has written, his wife "had become unresponsive, grudging, inert, close to inhuman."[56]

Emma Darwin, like Catherine Dickens, grew old and shapeless. And Charles Darwin, like Charles Dickens, rose markedly in stature after his wedding. But there's no evidence that Darwin ever saw Emma as close to inhuman. What accounts for the difference?

Chapter 6: **THE DARWIN PLAN FOR MARITAL BLISS**

She has been my greatest blessing, and I can declare that in my whole life I have never heard her utter one word which I had rather have been unsaid. . . . She has been my wise adviser and cheerful comforter throughout life, which without her would have been during a very long period a miserable one from ill-health. She has earned the love and admiration of every soul near her.

—*Autobiography* (1876)[1]

In his pursuit of a lasting and fulfilling marriage, Charles Darwin possessed several distinct advantages.

To begin with, there was his chronic ill health. Nine years into marriage, while visiting his ailing father, and while ailing himself, he wrote to Emma of how he "yearned" for her, as "without you, when sick I feel most desolate." He closed the letter: "I do long to be with you & under your protection for then I feel safe."[2] After three decades of marriage, Emma would observe that "nothing marries one so completely as sickness."[3] This reflection may have been more bitter than sweet; Darwin's illness was a lifelong burden for her, and she couldn't have grasped its full weight until well after the wedding. But, whether or not it gave her second thoughts about the marriage, it meant that, for much of Darwin's married life, he wasn't a very marketable commodity. And in marriage, an unmarketable commodity—male or female—is often a contented one, with little if any sexual restlessness.

A complementary asset that Darwin brought to his marriage was hearty subscription to the Victorian ideal of woman as spiritual salvation. In his premarital deliberative soliloquies, he had imagined an "angel" who would keep him industrious yet not let him suffocate in his work. He got that, and a nurse too. And, for good measure, the chasteness of the courtship may have helped keep Emma filed under "Madonna" in Darwin's mind. Something did. "I marvel at my good fortune," he wrote toward the end of his life, "that she, so infinitely my superior in every single moral quality, consented to be my wife."[4]

A third advantage was residential geography. The Darwins lived, gibbon-like, on an eighteen-acre parcel, two hours by coach from London and its young female distractions. Male sexual fantasies tend to be essentially visual in nature, whereas female fantasies more often include tender touching, soft murmurs, and other hints of future investment. Not surprisingly, male fantasies, and male sexual arousal, are also more easily activated by sheerly visual cues, by the mere sight of anonymous flesh.[5] So visual isolation is an especially good way to keep a man from thinking the thoughts that could lead to marital discontent, infidelity, or both.

Isolation is hard to come by these days, and not just because attractive young women no longer stay in their homes, barefoot and pregnant. Images of beautiful women are everywhere we look. The fact that they're two-dimensional doesn't mean they're inconsequential. Natural selection had no way of "anticipating" the invention of photography. In the ancestral environment, distinct images of many beautiful young women would have signified a (genetically) profitable alternative to monogamy, and it would have been adaptive for feelings to shift accordingly. One evolutionary psychologist has found that men shown pictures of *Playboy* models later describe themselves as less in love with their wives than do men shown other images. (Women shown pictures from *Playgirl* felt no such attitude adjustment toward spouses.)[6]

The Darwins also had the blessing of fecundity. A marriage that produces a steady stream of children, and has the resources to care for them, may dampen the wanderlust of both women and men. Wandering takes time and energy, both of which can be well invested in those endearing little vehicles of genetic transmission. That divorce does grow less likely as more children are born is sometimes taken to mean that couples choose to endure the pain of matrimony "for the sake of children." No doubt this happens. But it's at least possible that evolution has inclined us to love a mate more deeply when marriage proves fruitful.[7] In either event, couples who say they'll stay married but won't have children may well prove wrong on one count or the other.[8]

We can now roughly sketch a Charles Darwin plan for marital bliss: have a chaste courtship, marry an angel, move to the country not long after the wedding, have tons of kids, and sink into a deeply debilitating illness. A heartfelt commitment to your work probably helps too, especially when the work doesn't entail business trips.

MARRIAGE TIPS FOR MEN

From the point of view of the average, late-twentieth-century man, the Darwin plan doesn't get high marks for feasibility. Perhaps some more practicable keys to lifelong monogamy can be gleaned from Darwin's life. Let's start with his three-step approach to marriage: (1) decide, rationally and systematically, to get married; (2) find someone who in most practical ways meets your needs; (3) marry her.

One biographer has chastised Darwin for this formulaic approach, complaining that "there is an emotional emptiness about his ponderings on marriage."[9] Maybe so. But it's worth noting that Darwin was a loving husband and father for around half a century. Any men who would like to fill this role might profit from looking closely at the "emotional emptiness" of Darwin's ruminations on marriage. They may hold a lesson transplantable to modern times.

Namely: lasting love is something a person has to *decide* to experience. Lifelong monogamous devotion is just not natural—not for women even, and emphatically not for men. It requires what, for lack of a better term, we can call an act of will. Hence the aptness of Darwin's apparent separation of the marriage question from the marriage-partner question. That he made up his mind—firmly, in the end—to get married and to make the most of his marriage was as important as his choice of mate.

This isn't to say that a young man can't hope to be seized by love. Darwin himself got fairly worked up by his wedding day. But whether the sheer fury of a man's feelings accurately gauges their likely endurance is another question. The ardor will surely fade, sooner or later, and the marriage will then live or die on respect, practical compatibility, simple affection, and (these days, especially) determination. With the help of these things, something worthy of the label "love" can last until death. But it will be a different kind of love from the kind that began the marriage. Will it be a richer love, a deeper love, a more spiritual love? Opinions vary. But it's certainly a more impressive love.

A corollary of the above is that marriages aren't made in heaven. One great spur to divorce is the belief of many men (and no few women) that somehow they just married the "wrong" person and next time they'll get it "right." Not likely. Divorce statistics support Samuel Johnson's characterization of a man's decision to remarry as "the triumph of hope over experience."[10]

John Stuart Mill held a similarly sober view. Mill insisted on *tolerance* of moral diversity, and stressed the long-term value of experimentation by society's nonconformists, but he didn't recommend moral adventurism as a lifestyle. Beneath the radicalism of *On Liberty* lay Mill's belief in keeping our impulses under firm cerebral control. "Most persons have but a very moderate capacity of happiness," he wrote in a letter. "Expecting . . . in marriage a far greater degree of happiness than they commonly find: and knowing not that the fault is in their own scanty capabilities of happiness—they fancy they should have been happier with some one else." His advice to the unhappy: sit still until the feeling passes. "[I]f they remain united, the feeling of disappointment after a time goes off, and they pass their lives together with fully as much happiness as they could find either singly or in any other union, without having undergone the wearing of repeated and unsuccessful experiments."[11]

Many men—and some, but fewer, women—would enjoy the opening stages of those experiments. But in the end they might find that the glimpse of lasting joy the second time around was just another delusion sponsored by their genes, whose primary goal, remember, is to make us prolific, not lastingly happy (and which, anyway, aren't operating in the environment of our design; in a modern society, where polygamy is illegal, a polygamous impulse can do more emotional damage to all concerned—notably offspring—than natural selection "intended"). The question then becomes whether the fleeting fun of greener pastures outweighs the pain caused by leaving the golden-brown ones. This isn't a simple question, much less a question whose answer is easy to impose on one's yearnings. But more often than many people (men in particular) care to admit, the answer is no.

And, anyway, there is debate over whether a minute-by-minute summation of pleasure and pain should settle the issue. Maybe the cumulative coherence of a life counts for something. Men from many generations have testified that over the long haul, a life shared with another person and several little people, for all its diverse frustrations, brings rewards of a sort unattainable through other means. Of course, we shouldn't give infinite weight to the testimony of old married men. For every one of them who claims to have had a fulfilling life, there is at least one bachelor claiming to be enjoying his series of conquests. But it's noteworthy that a number of these old men went through early phases of sexual liberty and concede that they enjoyed them. None of those making the other side of the argument can say they know what it's like to create a family and stay with it until the end.

John Stuart Mill made this point in a larger context. Even Mill, who, as the foremost publicist of utilitarianism, insisted that "pleasure, and freedom from pain, are the only things desirable as ends," didn't mean that the way it sounds. He believed that the pleasure and pain of all people affected by your actions (emphatically including any people your marriage created) belong in your moral calculus. Further, Mill stressed not just quantity of pleasure but quality, attaching special value to pleasures involving the "higher faculties." He wrote: "Few human creatures would consent to be changed into any of the lower animals, for a promise of the fullest allowance of a beast's pleasures. . . . It is better to be a human being dissatisfied than a pig satisfied; better to be Socrates dissatisfied than a fool satisfied. And if the fool, or the pig, is of a different opinion, it is because they only know their own side of the question. The other party to the comparison knows both sides."[12]

DIVORCE THEN AND NOW

Since Darwin's day, the incentive structure surrounding marriage has been transformed—indeed, inverted. Back then men had several good reasons to get married (sex, love, and societal pressure) and a good reason to stay married (they had no choice). Today an unmarried man can get sex, with or without love, regularly and respectably. And if for some reason he does stumble into matrimony, there's no cause for alarm; when the thrill is gone, he can just move out of the house and resume an active sex life without raising local eyebrows. The ensuing divorce is fairly simple. Whereas Victorian marriage was enticing and ultimately entrapping, modern marriage is unnecessary and eminently escapable.

This change had begun by the turn of the century, and it reached dramatic proportions after midcentury. The American divorce rate, which was level during the 1950s and early 1960s, doubled between 1966 and 1978, reaching its present level. Meanwhile, as escape from marriage became simple and commonplace, the incentive for men (and, in a probably less dramatic way, for women) to enter one was being dulled. Between 1970 and 1988, though the average age of a woman upon (first) marriage was rising, the number of eighteen-year-old girls who reported having had intercourse grew from 39 to 70 percent. For fifteen-year-olds it went from one in twenty to one in four.[13] The number of unmarried couples living together in the United States grew from half a million in 1970 to nearly three million in 1990.

Hence the double whammy: as easy divorce creates a growing population of formerly married women, easy sex creates a growing population of never-married women. Between 1970 and 1990, the number of American women aged thirty-five to thirty-nine who had never been married rose from one in twenty to one in ten.[14] And of women in that age group who *have* gotten married, about a third have also gotten divorced.[15]

For men, the figures are even more severe. One in seven men aged thirty-five to thirty-nine has never married; as we've seen, serial monogamy tends to leave more men than women in that condition.[16] Still, women may be the bigger losers here. They are more likely than men to want children, and a forty-year-old unmarried childless woman, unlike her male counterpart, is watching her chances of parenthood head briskly toward zero. And as for the relative fortunes of *formerly* married men and women: in the United States, divorce brings the average man a marked increase in standard of living, while his wife, along with her children, suffers the opposite.[17]

The Divorce Act of 1857, which helped legitimize marital breakup in England, was welcomed by many feminists. Among them was John Stuart Mill's wife, Harriet Taylor Mill, who, until the death of her first husband, had been trapped in a marriage she detested. Mrs. Mill, who seems never to have been a great enthusiast for sexual intercourse, had painfully come to believe "that all men, with the exception of a few lofty minded, are sensualists more or less" and that "women on the contrary are quite exempt from this trait." To any wife who shared her distaste for sex, Victorian marriage could seem like a series of rapes punctuated by dread. She favored divorce on demand for the sake of women.

Mill too favored divorce on demand (*assuming* the couple had no children). But his view of the matter differed from hers. He saw wedding vows as a constraint less on the wife than on the husband. The strict marriage laws of the day, Mill observed, with great insight into the likely origins of institutionalized monogamy, had been written "*by* sensualists, *for* sensualists, and *to bind* sensualists."[18] He was not alone in this view. Behind opposition to the Divorce Act of 1857 was a fear that it would turn men into serial monogamists. Gladstone opposed the bill because, he said, it "would lead to the degradation of woman."[19] (Or, as an Irish woman would put it more than a century later: "A woman voting for divorce is like a turkey voting for Christmas.")[20] The effects of easy divorce have been complex, but in many ways the evidence supports Gladstone. Divorce is very often a raw deal for women.

There's no point in trying to turn back the clock, no point in trying to sustain marriages by making the alternative virtually illegal. Studies show that the one thing harder on children than divorce is for parents to stay together even though locked in mortal combat.

But surely there shouldn't be a financial *incentive* for a man to get divorced; divorce shouldn't *raise* his personal standard of living, as it now usually does. In fact, it seems only fair to lower his standard of living—not necessarily to punish him, but because that's often the only way to keep the living standards of his wife and children from plunging, given the inefficiencies of two households compared to one. If financially secure, women can often be happy rearing children without a man—happier than they were with him, sometimes, and happier even than he'll be after he's gotten used to the grass on the other side of the fence.

R-E-S-P-E-C-T

There is a difference of opinion over how much "respect" women get in the modern moral climate. Men think they get lots. The portion of American men saying women are better respected than in the past went from 40 percent in 1970 to 62 percent in 1990. Women disagree. In a 1970 survey, they were most likely to call men "basically kind, gentle, and thoughtful," but a 1990 survey conducted by the same pollster found women most likely to describe men as valuing only their own opinions, trying to keep women down, preoccupied with getting women into bed, and not paying attention to household affairs.[21]

Respect is an ambiguous word. Maybe those men who consider women well "respected" mean that women have been accepted at work as worthy colleagues. And maybe women are indeed getting more of this kind of respect. But if by *respect* you mean what the Victorians meant when they urged respect for women—not treating them as objects of sexual conquest—then respect has probably dropped since 1970 (and it certainly has since 1960). One interpretation of the above numbers is that women would like to have more of this second kind of respect.

There's no clear reason for a sharp trade-off between the two; no reason that feminists of the late 1960s and early 1970s, in insisting on the first kind of respect, had to undermine the second (which, actually, they said they also wanted). But, as things happened, they did. They preached the innate symmetry of the sexes in all major arenas, including sex. Many young women took the doctrine of symmetry to mean they could follow their sexual attractions and disregard any vague visceral wariness: sleep with any man they liked, without fear that his sexual interest didn't signify comparable affection, without fear that sex might be more emotionally entangling for her than for him. (Some feminists practiced casual sex almost out of a sense of ideological commitment.) Men, for their part, used the doctrine of symmetry to ease themselves off the moral hook. Now they could sleep around without worrying about the emotional fallout; women were just like them, so no special consideration was necessary. In this they were, and are, aided by women who actively resist special moral consideration as patronizing (which it sometimes is, and certainly was in Victorian England).

Lawmakers, meanwhile, took sexual symmetry to mean that women needed no special legal protection.[22] In many states, the 1970s brought "no-fault" divorce and the automatically equal division of a couple's assets—even if one spouse, usually the wife, hasn't been on a career track and thus faces bleaker prospects. The lifelong alimony that a divorced woman could once expect may now be replaced by a few years of "rehabilitative maintenance" payments, which are supposed to give her time to launch her career recovery—a recovery that, in fact, will extend beyond a few years if she has a few children to tend. In trying to get a more equitable deal, it won't help to point out that the cause of the breakup was her husband's rampant philandering, or his sudden, brutal intolerance. These things, after all, are nobody's fault. The no-fault philosophy is one reason divorce is literally a profitable enterprise for men. (The other reason is lax enforcement of the man's financial obligations.) The height of the no-fault vogue has now passed, and state legislatures have undone some of the damage, but not all.

The feminist doctrine of innate sexual symmetry wasn't the only culprit, or even, initially, the main one. Sexual and marital norms had been changing for a long time, for many reasons, ranging from contraceptive technology to communications technology, from residential patterns to recreational trends. So why dwell on feminism?

Partly because of the sheer irony that (perfectly laudable) attempts to stop one kind of exploitation of women aided another kind. Partly, too, because, though feminists didn't single-handedly create the problem, some of them have helped sustain it. Until very recently, fear of feminist backlash was far and away the main obstacle to an honest discussion of differences between the sexes. Feminists have written articles and books denouncing "biological determinism" without bothering to understand biology or determinism. And the increasing, if belated, feminist discussion of sex differences is sometimes vague and disingenuous; there is a tendency to describe differences that are plausibly explicable in Darwinian terms while dodging the question of whether they are innate.[23]

UNHAPPILY MARRIED WOMEN

The "Darwin plan" for staying married—and, indeed, the general thrust of this chapter so far—may seem to presuppose a simple picture: women love marriage, men don't. Obviously, life is more complicated than that. Some women don't want to get married, and many more, once married, are far from bliss. If this chapter has stressed the *male* mind's incongruence with monogamous marriage (and it has), it's not because I think the female mind is a perpetual font of adulation and fidelity. It's because I think the male mind is the largest single obstacle to lifelong monogamy—and certainly the largest such obstacle that emerges distinctly from the new Darwinian paradigm.

The incongruence between the *female* mind and modern marriage is less simple and clear-cut (and, in the end, less disruptive). The clash isn't so much with monogamy itself as with the social and economic setting of modern monogamy. In the typical hunter-gatherer society, women have both a working life and a home life, and reconciling the two isn't hard. When they go out to gather food, child care is barely an issue; their children may go with them or, instead, stay with aunts, uncles, grandparents, cousins. And when mothers, back from work, do care for children, the context is social, even communal. The anthropologist Marjorie Shostak, after living in an African hunter-gatherer village, wrote: "The isolated mother burdened with bored small children is not a scene that has parallels in !Kung daily life."[24]

Most modern mothers seem to find themselves well to one side or the other of the (reasonably) happy medium that a hunter-gatherer woman naturally strikes. They may work forty or fifty hours a week, worry about the quality of day care, and feel vaguely guilty. Or they may be full-time housewives who rear their children alone and are driven nearly mad by monotony. Some housewives, of course, manage to build a solid social infrastructure even amid the transience and anonymity of the typical modern neighborhood. But the unhappiness of the many women who don't is virtually inevitable. It's no surprise that modern feminism gathered such momentum during the 1960s, after post–World War II suburbanization (and so much else) had diluted the sense of neighborhood community and pulled the extended family apart; women weren't designed to be suburban housewives.

The generic suburban habitat of the fifties was more "natural" for men. Like many hunter-gatherer fathers, vintage suburban husbands spent a little time with their children and a lot of time out bonding with males, in work, play, or ritual.[25] For that matter, many Victorian men (though not Darwin) had the same setup. Although lifelong monogamy per se is less natural for men than for women, one form that monogamous marriage has often taken, and still often takes, may be harder on women than on men.

But that's not the same as saying that the female mind threatens modern monogamy more than, or as much as, the male mind. A mother's discontent seems not to translate into breakup as naturally as a father's. The ultimate reason is that, in the ancestral environment, seeking a new husband once there were children was seldom a genetically winning proposition.

To make modern monogamy "work"—in the sense both of enduring and of leaving husband and wife fairly happy—is a challenge of overwhelming complexity. A successful overhaul might well entail tampering with the very structure of modern residential and vocational life. Any aspiring tamperers would do well to ponder the social environment in which human beings evolved.

People weren't, of course, designed to be relentlessly happy in the ancestral environment; there, as here, anxiety was a chronic motivator, and happiness was the always pursued, often receding, goal. Still, people *were* designed not to go crazy in the ancestral environment.

THE EMMA PLAN

Notwithstanding the discontents of modern marriage, many women aspire to find a lifelong mate and have children. Given that the current climate doesn't favor this goal, what are they to do? We've talked about how men might behave if they want marriage to be a sturdier institution. But giving men marriage tips is a little like offering Vikings a free booklet titled "How Not to Pillage." If women are closer than men to being naturally monogamous, and often suffer from divorce, maybe they are a more logical locus for reform. As George Williams and Robert Trivers discovered, much of human sexual psychology flows from the scarceness of eggs relative to sperm. This scarcity gives women more power—in individual relationships, and in shaping the moral fabric—than they sometimes realize.

Sometimes they do realize it. Women who would like a husband and children have been known to try the Emma Wedgwood plan for landing a man. In its most extreme form, the plan runs as follows: if you want to hear vows of eternal devotion right up to your wedding day—and if you want to make sure there *is* a wedding day—don't sleep with your man until the honeymoon.

The idea here isn't just that, as the saying goes, a man won't buy the cow if he can get the milk for free. If the Madonna-whore dichotomy is indeed rooted firmly in the male mind, then early sex with a woman may tend to stifle any budding feelings of love for her. And, if there are such things as "mate-ejection modules" in the human mind, sustained sex without issue may bring—in the man *or* the woman—a cooling toward the other.

Many women find the Emma strategy abhorrent. To "trap" a man, some say, is beneath their dignity; if he has to be coerced into marriage, they'd rather do without him. Others say the Emma approach is reactionary and sexist, a revival of the hoary demand that women carry the moral burden of self-control for the sake of the social order. Still others say this approach seems to presume that sexual restraint for a woman is easy, which it often is not. These are all valid reactions.

There is one other common complaint about the Emma strategy: it doesn't work. These days much sex is available to men for little commitment. Not as much as a few years ago, maybe, but enough so that, if any one woman cuts off the supply, alternatives abound. Prim women sit at home alone and bask in their purity. Around Valentine's Day of 1992, the *New York Times* quoted a twenty-eight-year-old single woman who "lamented the lack of romance and courtship." She said, "Guys still figure if you don't come across, someone else will. It's like there's no incentive to wait until you get to know each other better."[26]

This, too, is a valid point, and a good reason why a one-woman austerity crusade isn't likely to bring great rewards. Still, some women have found that a move *of some distance* toward austerity may make sense.[27] If a man isn't interested enough in a woman, as a human being, to endure, say, two months of merely affectionate contact before graduating to lust, he's unlikely to stick around for long in any event. Some women have decided not to waste the time—which, needless to say, is more precious for them than for men.

This mild version of the Emma approach can be self-reinforcing. As more women discover the value of a short cooling-off period, it becomes easier for each of them to impose a longer one. If an eight-week wait is common, then a ten-week wait won't put a woman at much of a competitive disadvantage. Don't expect this trend to reach Victorian extremes. Women, after all, do like sex. But expect the trend, which seems already to be under way, to continue. Much of today's incipiently conservative sexual climate may come from a fear of sexually transmitted diseases; but, to judge by the increasingly clear opinion of many women that men are basically pigs, a part of the new climate may come from women rationally pursuing self-interest in recognition of harsh truths about human nature. And one generally safe bet is that people will continue to pursue their self-interest as they see it. In this case, evolutionary psychology helps them see it.

A THEORY OF MORAL CHANGE

There is another reason trends in sexual morality—whether toward or away from sexual reserve—may be self-sustaining. If men and women are indeed designed to tailor their sexual strategies to local market conditions, the norm among each sex depends on the norm among the other. We've already seen evidence, from David Buss and others, that when men deem a woman promiscuous, they treat her accordingly—as a short-term conquest, not a long-term prize. We've also seen evidence, from Elizabeth Cashdan, that women who perceive males to be generally pursuing short-term strategies are themselves more likely to look and act promiscuous: to wear sexy clothes and have sex often.[28] One can imagine these two tendencies getting locked in a spiral of positive feedback, leading to what the Victorians would have called ongoing moral decline. A proliferation of low-cut dresses and come-hither looks might send the visual cues that discourage male commitment; and as men, thus discouraged, grow less deferential toward women, and more overtly sexual, low-cut dresses might further proliferate. (Even come-hither looks that show up on billboards, or in the pages of *Playboy*, might have some effect.)[29]

If things should for some reason begin moving in the other direction, *toward* male parental investment, the trend could be sustained by the same dynamic of mutual reinforcement. The more Madonnaish the women, the more daddish and less caddish the men, and thus the more Madonnaish the women, and so on.

To call this theory speculative would almost be an understatement. It has the added disadvantage of being (like many theories of cultural change) hard to test directly. But it does rest on theories of individual psychology that are themselves testable. The Buss and Cashdan studies amount to a preliminary test, and so far the two pillars of the theory hold up. The theory also has the virtue of helping to explain why trends in sexual morality persist for so long. Just as Victorian prudishness, at its high-water mark, was the culmination of a century-long trend, it seems to have then receded for a long, long time.

Why does the long, slow swing of the pendulum ever reverse? The possible reasons range from changes in technology (contraceptive, for example) to changes in demographics.[30] It's possible too that the pendulum may tend to reverse when a large fraction of one sex or the other (or both) finds its deepest interests not being served and begins to consciously reevaluate its lifestyle. In 1977 Lawrence Stone observed, "The historical record suggests that the likelihood of this period of extreme sexual permissiveness continuing for very long without generating a strong backlash is not very great. It is an ironic thought that just at the moment when some thinkers are heralding the advent of the perfect marriage based on full satisfaction of the sexual, emotional and creative needs of both husband and wife, the proportion of marital breakdowns, as measured by the divorce rate, is rising rapidly."[31] Since he wrote, women, who have much leverage over sexual morality, have, in apparently growing numbers, asked basic questions about the wisdom of highly casual sex. Whether we are entering a period of long growth in moral conservatism is impossible to say. But modern society doesn't exude an overwhelming sense of satisfaction with the status quo.

VICTORIA'S SECRET

Many judgments have been rendered about Victorian sexual morality. One is that it was horribly and painfully repressive. Another is that it was well suited to the task of preserving marriage. Darwinism affirms these two judgments and unites them. Once you have seen the odds against lifelong monogamous marriage, especially in an economically stratified society—in other words, once you have seen human nature—it is hard to imagine anything short of harsh repression preserving the institution.

But Victorianism went well beyond simple, general repression. Its particular inhibitions were strikingly well-tailored to the task at hand.

Perhaps the greatest threat to lasting marriage—the temptation of aging, affluent, or high-status men to desert their wives for a younger model—was met with great social firepower. Though Charles Dickens did manage, amid great controversy and at real social cost, to leave his wife, he forever confined contact with his mistress to secret meetings. To admit that his desertion was, in fact, a desertion would have been to draw a censure he wasn't willing to face.

It's true that some husbands spent time in one or another of London's many brothels (and housemaids sometimes served as sexual outlets for men of the upper classes). But it's also true that male infidelity may not threaten marriage so long as it doesn't lead to desertion; women, more easily than men, can reconcile themselves to living with a mate who has cheated. And one way to ensure that male infidelity doesn't lead to desertion is to confine it to, well, whores. We can safely bet that few Victorian men sat at the breakfast table daydreaming about leaving their wives for the prostitute they had enjoyed the night before; and we can speculate with some confidence that part of the reason is a Madonna-whore dichotomy planted deeply in the male psyche.

If a Victorian man did more directly threaten the institution of monogamy, if he committed adultery with "respectable" women, the risk was great. Darwin's physician, Edward Lane, was accused in court by a patient's husband of committing adultery with the patient. In those days, this sort of case was so scandalous that the *Times* of London carried daily coverage. Darwin followed it closely. Perhaps conveniently, he doubted Lane's guilt ("I never heard a sensual expression from him"), and he worried about Lane's future: "I fear it will ruin him."[32] It probably would have, if the judge hadn't exonerated him.

Of course, in keeping with the double standard, female adulterers drew even stronger censure than their male counterparts. Both Lane and his patient were married, yet her diary recounted a post-tryst conversation between them that allocated blame in the following proportions. "I entreated him to believe that since my marriage I had never before in the smallest degree transgressed. He consoled me for what I had done, and conjured me to forgive myself."[33] (Lane's lawyer convinced the court that her diary was a mad fantasy, but even if so, it reflects prevailing morality.)

The double standard may not be fair, but it does have a kind of rationale. Adultery per se is a greater threat to monogamy when the wife commits it. (Again: the average man will have much more trouble than the average woman continuing a marriage with a mate known to have been unfaithful.) And if the husband of an adulterer does for some reason stay in the marriage, he may start treating the children less warmly, now that doubts about their paternity have arisen.

Conducting this sort of brisk, clinical appraisal of Victorian morality is risky. People are inclined to misunderstand. So let's be clear: clinical isn't the same as prescriptive; this is *not* an argument on behalf of the double standard, or any other particular aspect of Victorian morality.

Indeed, whatever contribution the double standard may have once made to marital stability by offering a vent for male lust, times have changed. These days a high-powered businessman doesn't confine his extramarital affairs to prostitutes, or to maids and secretaries whose cultural backgrounds make them unlikely wives. With women more widely in the workplace, he will meet young single women at the office, or on a business trip, who are exactly the sort he might marry if he had it to do all over again; and he *can* do it all over again. Whereas extramarital activity in the nineteenth century, and often in the 1950s, was a sheerly sexual outlet for an otherwise committed husband, today it is often a slippery slope toward desertion. The double standard may have once bolstered monogamy, but these days it brings divorce.

Even aside from the question of whether Victorian morality would "work" today, there is the question of whether any benefits would justify its many peculiar costs. Some Victorian men and women felt desperately trapped by marriage. (Although when marriages seem inescapable, almost literally unthinkable, people may dwell less on shortcomings.) And prevailing morality made it hard for some women to guiltlessly enjoy even marital sex—not to mention the fact that Victorian men weren't known for their sexual sensitivity. Life was also hard for women who wanted to be more than ornaments, more than an "Angel in the House." The Darwin sisters reported to Charles with some concern about brother Erasmus's budding, if ambiguous, friendship with the author Harriet Martineau, who didn't fit meekly into the feminine mold. Darwin, upon meeting her, had this impression: "She was very agreeable and managed to talk on a most wonderful number of subjects, considering the limited time. I was astonished to find how little ugly she is, but as it appears to me, she is overwhelmed with her own projects, her own thoughts and own abilities. Erasmus palliated all this, by maintaining one ought not to look at her as a woman."[34] This sort of remark is one of many reasons we shouldn't try to recreate Victorian sexual morality wholesale.

There no doubt are other moral systems that could succeed in sustaining monogamous marriage. But it seems likely that any such system will, like Victorianism, entail real costs. And although we can certainly strive for a morality that distributes costs *evenly* between men and women (and evenly among men and among women), distributing the costs *identically* is less likely. Men and women are different, and the threats that their evolved minds pose to marriage are different. The sanctions with which an efficient morality combats these threats will thus be different for the two sexes.

If we are really serious about restoring the institution of monogamy, *combat*, it seems, will indeed be the operative word. In 1966, one American scholar, looking back at the sense of shame surrounding the sexual impulse among Victorian men, discerned "a pitiable alienation on the part of a whole class of men from their own sexuality."[35] He's certainly right about the alienation. But the "pitiable" part is another question. At the other end of the spectrum from "alienation" is "indulgence"—obedience to our sexual impulses as if they were the voice of the Noble Savage, a voice that could restore us to some state of primitive bliss which, in fact, never was. A quarter-century of indulging these impulses has helped bring a world featuring, among other things: lots of fatherless children; lots of embittered women; lots of complaints about date rape and sexual harassment; and the frequent sight of lonely men renting X-rated videotapes while lonely women abound. It seems harder these days to declare the Victorian war against male lust "pitiable." Pitiable compared to what? Samuel Smiles may seem to have been asking a lot when he talked about spending one's life "armed against the temptation of low indulgences," but the alternative isn't obviously preferable.

WHERE DO MORAL CODES COME FROM?

The intermittently moralistic tone of this chapter is in a sense ironic. Yes, on the one hand, the new Darwinian paradigm does suggest that any institution as "unnatural" as monogamous marriage may be hard to sustain without a strong (that is, repressive) moral code. But the new paradigm also has a countervailing effect: nourishing a certain moral relativism—if not, indeed, an outright cynicism about moral codes in general.

The closest thing to a generic Darwinian view of how moral codes arise is this: people tend to pass the sorts of moral judgments that help move their genes into the next generation (or, at least, the kinds of judgments that would have furthered that cause in the environment of our evolution). Thus a moral code is an informal compromise among competing spheres of genetic self-interest, each acting to mold the code to its own ends, using any levers at its disposal.[36]

Consider the sexual double standard. The most obvious Darwinian explanation is that men were designed, on the one hand, to be sexually loose themselves yet, on the other, to relegate sexually loose women ("whores") to low moral status—even, remarkably, as those same men encourage those same women to be sexually loose. Thus, to the extent that men shape the moral code, it may include a double standard. Yet on closer inspection, this quintessentially male judgment is seen to draw natural support from other circles: the parents of young, pretty girls, who encourage their daughters to save their favors for Mr. Right (that is, to remain attractive targets for male parental investment), and who tell their daughters it's "wrong" to do otherwise; the daughters themselves, who, while saving their virtue for a high bidder, self-servingly and moralistically disparage the competing, low-rent alternatives; happily married women who consider an atmosphere of promiscuity a clear and present danger to their marriage (that is, to continued high investment in their offspring). There is a virtual genetic conspiracy to depict sexually loose women as evil. Meanwhile, there is relative tolerance for male philandering, and not only because some males (especially attractive or rich ones) may themselves like the idea. Wives, too, by finding a husband's desertion more shattering than his mere infidelity, reinforce the double standard.

If you buy this way of looking at moral codes, you won't expect them to serve the interests of society at large. They emerge from an informal political process that presumably gives extra weight to powerful people; they are quite unlikely to represent everyone's interests equally (though more likely to do so, perhaps, in a society with free speech and economic equality). And there's definitely no reason to assume that existing moral codes reflect some higher truth apprehended via divine inspiration or detached philosophical inquiry.

Indeed, Darwinism can help highlight the contrast between the moral codes we have and the sort that a detached philosopher might arrive at. For example: though the double standard's harsh treatment of female promiscuity may be a natural by-product of human nature, an ethical philosopher might well argue that sexual license is more often *morally* dubious in the case of the man. Consider an unmarried man and an unmarried woman on their first date. The man is more likely than the woman to exaggerate emotional commitment (consciously or unconsciously) and obtain sex under these false pretenses. And, if he does so, his warmth is then more likely than hers to fade. This is far, far from a hard and fast rule; human behavior is very complex, situations and individuals vary greatly, and members of both sexes get emotionally chewed up in all kinds of ways. Still, as a gross generalization, it is probably fair to say that single men cause more pain to partners of short duration through dishonesty than single women do. So long as women don't sleep with already mated men, their sexual looseness typically harms others obliquely and diffusely, if at all. Thus, if you believe, as most people seem to, that it is immoral to cause others pain by implicitly or explicitly misleading them, you might be more inclined to condemn the sexual looseness of men than of women.

That, at any rate, would be my inclination. If in this chapter I seemed to suggest that women practice sexual restraint, the advice wasn't meant to carry any overtone of obligation. It was self-help, not moral philosophy.

This may sound paradoxical: one can, from a Darwinian vantage point, advise sexual restraint for women, roughly echoing traditional moral exhortation, while at the same time decrying the moral censure of women who don't take the advice. But you might as well get used to the paradox, for it's part of a more general Darwinian slant on morality.

On the one hand, a Darwinian may treat existing morality with suspicion. On the other hand, traditional morality often embodies a certain utilitarian wisdom. After all, the pursuit of genetic interest sometimes, though not always, coincides with the pursuit of happiness. Those mothers who urge their daughters to "save themselves" may at one level be counseling ruthless genetic self-interest, but they are, on another level, concerned for the long-term happiness of their daughters. So too for the daughters who follow mother's advice, believing it will help them become lastingly married and have children: yes, the reason they want childen is because their genes "want" them to want children; nonetheless, the fact remains that they *do* want children, and may well, in fact, have more fulfilling lives if they get them. Though there's nothing inherently good about genetic self-interest, there's nothing inherently wrong with it either. When it does conduce to happiness (which it won't always), and doesn't gravely hurt anyone else, why fight it?

For the Darwinian inclined toward moral philosophy, then, the object of the game is to examine traditional morality under the assumption that it is laden with practical, life-enhancing wisdom, yet is also laced with self-serving and philosophically indefensible pronouncements about the absolute "immorality" of this or that. Mothers may be wise to counsel restraint in their daughters—and, for that matter, wise to condemn competing girls who aren't so restrained. But the claim that these condemnations have *moral* force may be just a bit of genetically orchestrated sophistry.

Extricating the wisdom from the sophistry will be the great and hard task of moral philosophers in the decades to come, assuming that more than a few of them ever get around to appreciating the new paradigm. It is a task, in any event, to which we'll return toward the end of this book, after the origins of the most fundamental moral impulses have become apparent.

SUGARCOATED SCIENCE

One common reaction to discussions of morality in light of the new Darwinism is: Aren't we getting a little ahead of the game here? Evolutionary psychology is just getting started. It has produced some theories with powerful support (an innate difference in male and female jealousy); some with fair-to-middling support (the Madonna-whore dichotomy); and many more that are sheer, if plausible, speculation (the "mate ejection" module). Is this body of theories really capable of supporting sweeping pronouncements about Victorian, or any other, morality?

Philip Kitcher, a philosopher who in the 1980s established himself as sociobiology's preeminent critic, has carried this doubt a step further. He believes Darwinians should tread carefully not just in making moral or political extensions from their inchoate science (extensions most of them avoid anyway, thanks to the scorching a few received in the 1970s), but in making the science in the first place. After all, even if they don't cross the line between science and values, someone else will; theories about human nature will inevitably be used to support this or that doctrine of morality or social policy. And if the theories turn out to be wrong, they may have done a lot of damage in the meanwhile. Social science, Kitcher notes, is different from physics or chemistry. If we embrace "an incorrect view of the origins of a distant galaxy," then "the mistake will not prove tragic. By contrast, if we are wrong about the bases of human social behavior, if we abandon the goal of a fair distribution of the benefits and burdens of society because we accept faulty hypotheses about ourselves and our evolutionary history, then the consequences of a scientific mistake may be grave indeed." Thus, "When scientific claims bear on matters of social policy, the standards of evidence and of self-criticism must be extremely high."[37]

There are two problems here. First, "self-criticism" per se is not an essential part of science. Criticism from colleagues—a kind of *collective* self-criticism—is. It is what keeps the "standards of evidence" high. And this collective self-criticism can't even begin until a hypothesis is put forward. Presumably Kitcher isn't suggesting that we short-circuit this algorithm of scientific progress by refraining

from the proposal of weak hypotheses; the way weak hypotheses get strong is by being proposed and then mercilessly scrutinized. And if Kitcher is suggesting only that we label speculative hypotheses as such, no one has any objection to that. Indeed, thanks to people like Kitcher (and this isn't meant sarcastically), many Darwinians are now masters of careful qualification.

Which brings us to the second problem with Kitcher's argument: the suggestion that Darwinian social scientists, but not social scientists generally, should proceed with great caution. The unspoken assumption is that incorrect Darwinian theories about behavior will tend to be more pernicious than incorrect *non*-Darwinian theories about behavior. But why should that be so? One long-standard and utterly non-Darwinian doctrine of psychology—that there are no important innate mental differences between men and women bearing on courtship and sex—seems to have caused a fair amount of suffering over the past few decades. And it depended on the lowest imaginable "standards of evidence"—no real evidence whatsoever, not to mention the blatant and arrogant disregard of folk wisdom in every culture on the planet. For some reason, though, Kitcher isn't upset about this; he seems to think that theories involving genes can have bad effects but theories not involving genes can't.

A more reliable generalization would seem to be that incorrect theories are more likely than correct theories to have bad effects. And if, as is often the case, we don't know for sure which theories are right and which are wrong, our best bet is to go with the ones that seem most likely to be right. The premise of this book is that evolutionary psychology, in spite of its youth, is now far and away the most likely source of theories about the human mind that will turn out to be right—and that, indeed, many of its specific theories already have fairly firm grounding.

Not all threats to the honest exploration of human nature come from the enemies of Darwinism. Within the new paradigm, truth sometimes gets sugarcoated. It is often tempting, for example, to downplay differences between men and women. Regarding the more polygamous nature of men, politically sensitive Darwinian social scientists may say things like: "Remember, these are only statistical generalizations, and any one person may diverge greatly from the

Emma and Charles Darwin around the time of their wedding. Evolutionary psychology sheds light on various aspects of their relationship, including Emma's relative coolness toward impending marriage. She wrote to Charles, "I shall always look upon the event of the 29th as a most happy one on my part though perhaps not so great or so good as you do."

Above: George Williams in the early 1960s. Williams helped formulate the theory that explains why in most species males are sexually assertive and females more reserved. He also saw a way to test the theory; if it is correct, then this pattern should be weak, or even reversed, in species whose males invest heavily in offspring. *Left:* A male seahorse gives birth after incubating eggs that the female laid in his pouch.

Above: The biologists Robert Trivers and John Maynard Smith in India in 1980. *Below:* A !Kung San father and daughter. In all human cultures, males invest heavily in offspring—less heavily than seahorse males, perhaps, but more heavily than males in the primate species most closely related to us. This male parental investment, Trivers has observed, helps explain much about human sexual psychology, including the kinds of duplicity to which men and women are prone.

!Kung San women collecting food. Hunter-gatherer societies are the closest thing we have to a real-life model of the social context of human evolution. These societies reconcile motherhood and work fairly simply, whether, as here, by bringing children to work or by using kin and friends for babysitting. The anthropologist Marjorie Shostak, who took this picture, wrote, "The isolated mother burdened with bored small children is not a scene that has parallels in !Kung daily life." Her remark illustrates a general point that may account for much current suffering: the human mind wasn't designed for the modern world.

Honeypot ants of the genus *Myrmecocystus,* hanging from the roof of an underground nest, their abdomens swollen with liquid food. During dry spells, these living storage bins provide nourishment for their relatives. Darwin successfully explained the utter altruism of sterile insect castes such as the honeypot, but in very vague terms. Only with the theory of kin selection in the early 1960s did biologists see that Darwin's logic could be used to explain self-sacrifice in many species, including ours.